*for Jim, + Joe*

New American and Canadian Poetry

*Merry Christmas*

*love*

*Stephen*

*1972*

# New American and Canadian Poetry

Edited and with an Introduction
## by John Gill

Beacon Press   Boston

# Contents

# Introduction

"So, what's new?" somebody says to me, casually or even with a certain amount of intensity. "What poets or schools of poetry are you talking about?"

And I immediately step back (in thought), get sly or gun-shy.

A lot of poets in the United States and Canada to choose from. A lot of them products of the writing schools. A lot of them miles away just writing say, "Fuck the schools." A lot of them dreaming of making it — that's a laugh: making the big-time as a poet. It's a bit like a girl picking up a snake. Now you've got it! What are you gonna do?

"So, what's new? I would seriously like to know."

Maybe you ought to read this book, first! . . . No! All right, then, I'll tell you. A lot since the last really good anthology racked it up. I mean *The New American Poetry, 1945–1960,* edited by Donald Allen.

For one thing, the kinds of poetry forming in the sixties have come and gone, even though they're still around. By this I mean the Black Mountain school à la Creeley and Olson; the New York school à la Koch and O'Hara; the Beats à la Corso and Ginsberg; and the Deep Image school à la Bly, Wright, and Merwin.

Of course the mere word "school," at least to American ears, has a dirty sound. So maybe it's not a bad thing to forget about schools — they're too handy a peg, anyway, to hang things on — whether it's the poet talking about what he writes and what is good or whether it's his followers trying to latch on to a tradition, a way of writing that will be valid. Schools imply a congregation all facing one way. Poets have to take what they can use from anywhere and go beyond it to create their poems. At best, schools are halfway houses, not homes.

There are no congregations in this anthology. At least I hope not. Maybe a trend or two, but nothing more. That doesn't mean that the poets in this anthology haven't learned anything from others. It simply means that the poets here are their own man and woman. In fact, if I were to insist upon anything it would be that the poets in *New American and Canadian Poetry* are themselves — when you read a Lyn Lifshin poem you know it's not a Marge Piercy poem or an Alden Nowlan poem. The American and Canadian poets here have reached themselves, and you, by direct proxy, reach yourself when you read them.

A poetry editor once said, "You like poems of direct statement, don't you?" He was unsure whether he was handing me a compliment or not. After all, direct statements can hardly be like poetic ones! I took it as a compliment, however. Poets are pretty direct — like a slash across the eyes: whips, cords, turkey feathers, apple blossoms! Poets are often so direct they have to couch it, guard it from the heat of the sun, from where distinctions break down and blurs begin. It's not the poets who see things "poetically." They wouldn't be caught dead doing it.

Poetic language (metaphoric language if you wish) is the most direct way of seeing and saying. Why do poets struggle to write poems? Surely not because they have flowery souls or because they're trying to escape. They're trying to get it down, directly-fully.

There are some who say that you have to strip language away, get rid of comparisons, of music, imagery, and so on. But why so conscious a striptease? Purification might be a fine impulse but to prescribe the purge means they or their language is sick and they are hollow-eyed for cure!

There are others who say the opposite: that the way to poetry is deep down in subconscious imagery where the well flows. But deep imagery is only as deep as the poet using it and begs the question: is there that much split between surface and depth that surface must be scorned for deeper connections? (Like separating body and soul all over again.) And Father Whitman is still laughing over that one.

The true situation is closer to the poets in this book. They use whatever they need for their poetry. They know what it means to be wealthy. They don't deny. It is true that modern poetry has learned a lot from prose. But the prosaic movement in poetry has been going on since, at least, Wordsworth. It's also true that the gift of metaphor is a rare one and that good imagery can't be manufactured. Good poetry is still good poetry. It has character. It throbs. It embarrasses. It might even be "obscene" to some. But I say, "Good. Right on!" And I hear Blake saying,

> Abstinence sows sand all over
> The ruddy limbs and flaming hair,
> But Desire gratified
> Plants fruits of life and beauty there.

A footnote:
It should be obvious to everyone who reads this book that Canadian poets are (1) fantastically good and (2) practically unknown in the States. Why? Because people read what is available. If American publishers are pretty stupid about American poets, they are literally blind to Canadian ones. So let me deplore blinders, borders, and publishing-promotion that ignores genuine art.

I would like to thank Ray Bentley, Beacon editor, for suggesting that I do this anthology and for helping me to carry it out.

Thanks also to the many poets who were interested in this anthology and who sent me manuscripts.

*Trumansburg, New York*                                John Gill
*January 1971*

Milton Acorn

Margaret Atwood, *photograph by Alan Walker*

Ken Belford

George Bowering

Aram Boyajian

Harley Elliott

Doug Fetherling

Ray Fraser

Len Gasparini, *photograph by Logan*

John Gill

Robert Hershon, *photograph by Robert Shapiro*

Geof Hewitt, *photograph by John Paul Lowens*

Emmett Jarrett, *photograph by Robert Shapiro*

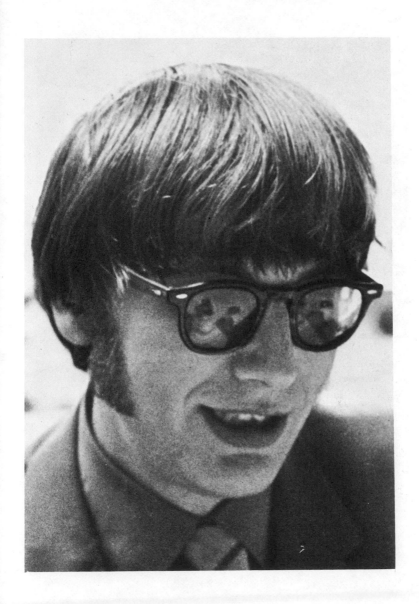

George Jonas

Patrick Lane, *photograph by Sheldon Grimson*

Irving Layton

Don L. Lee

Lyn Lifshin

Larry Mollin

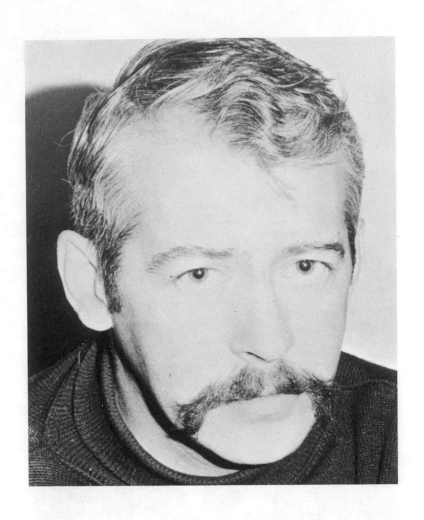

John Newlove, *photograph by Laurie English*

Alden Nowlan

Robert Peterson

Marge Piercy, *photograph by Robert Shapiro*

J. D. Reed

Dennis Saleh, *photograph by Robert T. McDonell*

Tom Schmidt

John Oliver Simon

Ian Young

# New American and Canadian Poetry

# Milton Acorn

## Blackfish Poem

Sunglare and sea pale as tears.
One long hour we watched the black whales
circling like dancers,
sliding dark backs out of water,
waving their heaved tails,
about an eyepupil-round spot
just a knife-edge
this side of the horizon.

## Offshore Breeze

The wind, heavy from the land, irons the surf
to a slosh on silver-damp sand.
The sea's grey and crocheted with ripples;
but shadows, the backs of waves,
lengthen and lapse in the dim haze,
hinting of farther, rougher doings.

The boats went out early, but now
come worm-slow thru haze and distance.
Their gunnels invisible, the men and engines
dots moving on a spit of foam,
they travel past my vision, past
that red jag of a headland, to harbor.

## I'd Like to Mark Myself

I'd like to mark myself
quiet, like one serene
calligraph in a color
so subtle it should only
be imagined (something

like a tree in winter
bear its lines and clusters
of snow, as if what's fallen
on it were its own).

I'd like to be quiet
except for a queer grin
that tells nothing but
whatever your own want
takes it as meaning.

But if I'm ever like that
don't believe me. You'll
know that I'm kind of
like a bud ... that I'm

waiting for the moment
when I can project
the tip of my tongue
and taste a raindrop

warm.


## Saint-Henri Spring

Spring I remember wild canaries,
gusts of dandelions
and green tongues of trees
in thoughts of shy ones.

Spring I see a rubber in the gutter,
a broom-handle on a mud lawn;
thaw-water trickles from a pyin udder.


2    *Milton Acorn*

I only see black petals
in the eyes of girls
self-contained as nettles,
choke-cherry sweet in hours
when even the slum grows flowers.

Spring I'm dwelt by startles of canaries,
coronal nudity
stuck to by drab threads of January.


## Monument

With gentleness
his eyes filmed
in his smile,
and he said

"The gaschamber boys
got my whole family;
I married
to give the vision
which is life
again to the line."

His son, with none
of life's handwriting
yet on his face,
played, and around him
the ghosts stood gossiping.


## I've Gone and Stained with the Color of Love

I've gone and stained with the color of love
The two hundred and fifty pound road foreman
Gone on his liquor, who sits
On my wicker armchair and strains it
So much in every binding point it can't even creak.

I've known him as a laugh-cursing soldier;
I've known him posed decisively as a statue
Out on the road, telling them what to do.
I've known him so much sufficing himself
Carrying his lunchpail . . .
                              But here he sits
And his eyes are like a bull's except
A bull's eyes don't hurt and his do . . .

Or does a bull cast such a poignant hurtful look
At the slaughterer between the blow and his collapse?
I've gone and stained with the color of love
Bulls too; and this man is called Bull . . .
He says to me, "Milt — You old bastard!"
And I say, "Bull — You old bastard!"
We've told each other about all our nicknames:
But his life was this — His Childhood and The War;
And all that followed was a disappointment.

I've gone and stained with the color of love
Life: — Well here is a man who knows life . . .
We tell each other about our wives
His dead, mine lost, his lost before her death:
And I say, "Bull, you old bastard!"
And he says, "Milt, you old bastard!"
It being the admission of manhood
That each have done wicked things.
So we pitch arguments back and forth;
But sometimes he just sits and watches me work.


**On Saint-Urbain Street**

My room's bigger than a coffin
but not so well made.
The couple on my left drink, and
at two a.m. the old man shouts
of going back to Russia.
About five he or his wrung-out wife
puke up their passage money.

The janitor (pay, five a week
plus a one-bed apartment
with furnace in kitchen) has
one laughing babe at home
and two girls, for lack of room,
in the orphanage.
On holidays they appear
with their soul-smashed faces.

Upstairs the Negro girl
answers the phone, sings my name
in a voice like a bad angel's.
Her boy-friends change
every week-end, like the movies.
But my room's cheap, tho
when the wind shifts north
I wear my overcoat
to type this bitter little poem.

## Ghostly Story

In winter twilight on a side street,
black — touched at the edges by snow,
with secondhand cars parked headlight to trunk,
a deadeye glow in each window,
I heard a "clip-clop," "clip-clop"
ringing as if the earth was hollow.

And all white with his tall ears
dusting the underside of heaven, a Clydesdale
with mighty brushes of hair on his hooves
swelled and swept from the shadows
. . . One moment I stood in his friendly eye
then like a lord he passed me.

With all the pride of his vanished race
he switched his big wind of a tail,
then turned a corner
and his hoofbeats abruptly stilled,
leaving one steaming brown bun
and a hush as if sparrows were listening.

## Lover That I Hope You Are

Lover that I hope you are . . . Do you need me?
For the vessel I am is like of a rare crystal
that must be full to will any giving. Only
such a choice at the same time is acceptance
as it is a demand high and arrogant.

Christ! I talk about love like a manoeuvre of
armored knights with drums and banners!
Is it for you whose least whisper against my skin
can twang me like a guitar-string? for
myself? or for something stronger than the saw
that cuts diamonds, yet is only a thought of perfection?

And this is not a guarantee, only a promise
made by one who can't judge either his weakness
or his strength . . . but must throw them
like dice, one who never intended to play
for small stakes, and who once having made the
        greatest gamble
and lost, lives for the next total throw.


## Poem for a Singer

Let me be the mane that swings
(clouds tossing, lightning-shot)
about the singer's muscled face,
caressing and letting it go wild.

Or let me be the oars' pulse
throbbing thru that figurehead
to the heroic Argo, that woman alive
who sang against the crash of spray

over her nipples, her chin,
and every love-wrought pore of her,
against the flattening calm, visions
washing up and down her spine.

I've tried to get that touch,
sufficient enough in myself to know
what's loved must fly its own directions
for sake of all my fantasies.

She sings and it seems to be my lips
which curl about a prisoner's curse,
I who watch while graves pop open
and the dead sing of how they've lived.

She sings in a crowded coffee shop,
smoke curling among tenuous ghosts
of the living: "Love!" she cries.
They scratch at love with palsied hands.

A pale assemblage of moons with no planet,
their mouths pluck as easily into a sneer
as to a yawn: "Sorrow!" cries the singer
. . . but their diluted tears . . .

"Courage!" cries the singer; but today
only the stupid or the very wise are brave.
"Justice!" Right now they won't be just
even to themselves, even to their souls

squirming like worms on a hook. No gods
they have but grey abstractions mulling
in the flaccid null-brain of Moloch: and
they live not by their own hopes but by his.

She sings as time and place have fated her
to people teetering on the last rung
of the last ladder down to the abyss;
who, one foot wavering down, feeling nothing

. . . feeling nothing but death for themselves,
desire the death of the entire world, because
even the imagination of life
is forbidden by all their teachers.

Let me be the song! Take me
as part of your beauty or an insult, like
a firebird above the last cloud of the last
dark planet, whose song of colored light

speeds into emptiness, creates emptiness,
transmogrifies emptiness to something like
itself, its sweet self. Oh let me be
that singer herself, with her guitar

crossed like a shield over her heart,
perched on this bomb of a world, every instant
ticking . . . ticking . . . Remembering,
remembering that she lives. Oh let me be

like the men and women of her song, those workers
who living in the very air made hideous
by the oppressor's breath, fought him
for every loose atom of their humanity. Oh let me

in these that might be the world's last days
be brave as they were, as the singer is . . . This heart
is necessary; even in the shadow
of Mount Death, it's necessary

: for the standing up proud and hopeful way, the
way expressing the truth of our lives,
we ought to die
is the only way we might live.

# Margaret Atwood

**Nine Untitled Poems**

**1**

I can change my-
self more easily
than I can change you

I could grow bark and
become a shrub

or switch back in time
to the woman image left
in cave rubble, the drowned
stomach bulbed with fertility,
face a tiny bead, a
lump, queen of the termites

or (better) speed myself up,
disguise myself in the knuckles
and purple-veined veils of old ladies,
become arthritic and genteel

or one twist further:
collapse across your
bed clutching my heart
and pull the nostalgic sheet up over
my waxed farewell smile

which would be inconvenient
but final.

**2**

In restaurants we argue
over which of us will pay for your funeral

though the real question is
whether or not I will make you immortal.

At the moment only I
can do it and so

I raise the magic fork
over the plate of beef fried rice

and plunge it into your heart.
There is a faint pop, a sizzle

and through your own split head
you rise up glowing;

the ceiling opens
a voice sings Love Is A Many

Splendoured Thing
you hang suspended above the city

in blue tights and a red cape,
your eyes flashing in unison.

The other diners regard you
some with awe, some only with boredom:

they cannot decide if you are a new weapon
or only a new advertisement.

As for me, I continue eating;
I liked you better the way you were,
but you were always ambitious.

**3**

After the agony in the guest
bedroom, you lying by the
overturned bed
your face uplifted, neck propped
against the windowsill, my arm
under you, cold moon
shining down through the window

wine mist rising
around you, an almost-
visible halo

You say, Do you
love me, do you love me

I answer you:
I stretch your arms out
one to either side,
your head slumps forward.

Later I take you home
in a taxi, and you
are sick in the bathtub.


**4**

You want to go back
to where the sky was inside us

animals ran through us, our hands
blessed and killed according to our
wisdom, death
made real blood come out

But face it, we have been
improved, our heads float
several inches above our necks
moored to us by
rubber tubes and filled with
clever bubbles,

                  our bodies
are populated with billions
of soft pink numbers
multiplying and analyzing
themselves, perfecting
their own demands, no trouble to anyone.

I love you by
sections and when you work.

Do you want to be illiterate?
This is the way it is, get used to it.

**5**

your back is rough all
over like a cat's tongue / I stroke
you lightly and you shiver

you clench yourself, withhold
even your flesh
outline / pleasure is what
you take but will not accept.

believe me, allow
me to touch you
gently, it may be the last

time / your closed eyes beat
against my fingers
I slip my hand down
your neck, rest on the pulse

you pull away

there is something in your throat that wants
to get out and you won't let it.

**6**

You refuse to own
yourself, you permit
others to do it for you:

you become slowly more public,
in a year there will be nothing left
of you but a megaphone

or you will descend through the roof
with the spurious authority of a
government official,
blue as a policeman, grey as a used angel,
having long forgotten the difference
between an annunciation and a parking ticket

or you will be slipped under
the door, your skin furred with cancelled
airmail stamps, your kiss no longer literature
but fine print, a set of instructions.

If you deny these uniforms
and choose to repossess
yourself, your future

will be less dignified, more painful, death will be sooner,
(it is no longer possible
to be both human and alive): lying piled with
the others, your face and body
covered so thickly with scars
only the eyes show through.

**7**

This year I intended children
a space where I could raise
foxes and strawberries, finally
be reconciled to fur seeds & burrows

but the entrails of dead cards
are against me, foretell
it will be water, the

element that shaped
me, that I shape by
being in

       It is the blue
cup, I fill it

it is the pond again
where the children, looking from
the side of the boat, see their mother

upside down, lifesize, hair streaming
over the slashed throat
and words fertilize each other
in the cold and with bulging eyes

**8**

We are standing facing each other
in an eighteenth century room
with fragile tables and mirrors
in carved frames; the curtains,
red brocade, are drawn

the doors are shut, you aren't talking,
the chandeliers aren't talking, the carpets

also remain silent.
You stay closed, your skin
is buttoned firmly around you,
your mouth is a tin decoration,
you are in the worst possible taste.

You are fake as the marble trim
around the fireplace, there is nothing
I wouldn't do to be away
from here.     I do nothing

because the light changes, the tables
and mirrors radiate from around you,
you step backwards away from me
the length of the room

holding cupped in your hands
behind your back
                              an offering
a gold word     a signal

I need more than
air, blood, it would open
everything

which you won't let me see.


**9**

Lying here, everything in me
brittle and pushing you away

This is not something I
wanted, I tell you

silently, not admitting
the truth of where

I am, so far
up, the sky incredible and dark

blue, each breath
a gift in the steep air

How hard even the boulders
find it to grow here

and I don't know how to accept
your freedom, I don't know

what to do with this
precipice, this joy

What do you see, I ask / my voice
absorbed by stone and outer

space / you are asleep, you see
what there is. Beside you

I bend and enter

# Ken Belford

## Beside the Road

There is a bale of hay
Beside the road
And rain drops on the window.

I can think of the time
I came down
From the Prairies on this road.

Me in the back seat,
Wearing a straw hat and beaded belt.
Thinking how hi the buildings are going to be.

The radio comes in for the first time
In one hundred and fifty miles
And it's playing the rolling home show.

But I'm going out
On the same road.
Only it's been paved since.

There is a bale of hay
Beside the road,
And no turning sideways now.

## Stove

It is an old stove.
Twisted. Cracked. Held together somehow
With baling wire and coat hangers.

And the four of us sitting around it,
With nothing encouraging to say
As we talk about the women we've laid.

Occasionally, one of us
Getting up, stoking the fire,
Sitting down again.

And it's this broken thing we have to keep going
That sits in between us
I've been wondering about.

## Dusk

From an old man
In an Autumn garden,
I learned how to get all the vegetables in.

Look again.
It is not a blue sky or colored like the sea.
It is of things much darker.

It is an anguished sky
That passes over the moon
And it makes me nervous.

He is still alive I hear.
Cutting brush every day
And folding his clothes carefully.

## Peanuts

Old Ernie Anderson eating peanuts.
Buying another old car each month, tying it together
With baling wire and driving the hell out of it.

Ernie with his ugly wife in the mornings,
Silent on his way to work. Bowling
Evenings with the kids when he would rather drink beer.

Or drinking with me. And between us the sorry references.
And getting drunk.
And spilling his brains over his nose.

Driving home fighting the wheel, driving
Down the middle of the road, coming
Home two hours late for supper.

Cussing like hell or shit.
Damning the foreman. Back wheels spinning out,
And pulling his brains back behind his eyes.

Looking sober in time for supper.
Ernie pitching his dirty coveralls after work.
Eating peanuts and throwing the shells.

## Branches Back Into

His job was
to walk in
front of me, I
can remember the sharp swing

of the wet swollen
branches back into
my face, feel it now,
now as the
skin rises,

can feel the
sudden white lines
they made on my skin, as
I followed him, holding
my end of the chain

in the one hand, in
the other, a
small axe for
notching
the trees.   No

one has since
followed us, or
built the road
it was to
be, be. I

can remember
falling, waist deep
in muskeg water, remember
only the outline
of his back

ahead of me, not
seeing the mountains
we were in:    they
were unimaginable,
exceed me.

Remember few words
passed between us, he
ahead of me
with his instruments
recording it all,

can remember, too, how
I answered him,
never once faltering,
shouting, even
though long

ago I had lost
my axe and was
too afraid
to tell him.

**For Kelley**

Take a look, i
sd, i sat
there

singing, dumb-
ly, as all
things

do, alone.
And i sat there
as long as

you, a sound
became
a breath

to me, saying
the same
dumb

sound
over and
over,


**8**

Hunchbacked and corrected,
I watched him limping
through the snow,
straining, he came the way to talk.

Three months and
today you write.
But there are worse exiles
than love
or the emptiness carved.

Not unlike the axolotl,
I have thought
my self into this,
even to the point of
being able to breed.

And I have slept
beneath these stones,
beneath these bones,
and I have felt
the earth turning;

it was turning
to the right
and folding into itself,

**New Potatoes**

The fiction of relationship:
It is cold.    In this weather
Things break.
The road signs are painted black.

In the root cellar,
The potatoes are
Growing their skins
Thicker, white roots sprouting hopelessly

Into darkness, into
Rootlessness.    As I do,
As you do.
I had a brother once,

In one other time.
Who was he
Whose skin was less
The outer layer,

And who, even
In the surest weather,
Wore his clothes long
And deep

Lest others see
The curious quick welts
Left from even
The most casual touch?


## Glove Glue

The soldier is
all alone, with
no company.   The
soldier is all alone,
with no
company.

When it is too late
to see, and the length of it all
seems hopeless, then
nothing in my body escapes me,
and i drift out of hope,
horizontally.
Let the horses run home.
I waited for you all
day.   Too bad
we missed
each other.
Impossible
as a fly with hipwaders.
Like we always do.   You
coughing.   Me
hearing it.   No point
to my story, no
point.   You coughing.
Me hearing it.

**2**

In spots
it is warm enough
and in those spots
it is a good knot I tie.
Otherwise, it is winter.

And, in winter,
it is always one day from spring.

With women,
it is always a false thaw.

On the river
ice to the horses
I am
with my bucket
of oats.
There are no gardeners
in the forest
and these are not
the only tracks
I discover.

So I lay my ear
down along the cold
steel rail to hear
something of her passage:
there was nothing.

**Blueline**

Sure as hell,
thrashing about
like this,

it makes the leaves
stiff, and the skin
stick.

Shoreline, shoreline,
you're all,
I know.

Go look in the water
and I'll show you
mine too.

Tiles on the floor
and the floor boards
rotten:

shoreline, shoreline,
every time
the train

goes by
the whole
house shakes.

# George Bowering

**The Egg**

The egg sat on the workbench
for weeks, me passing it every day
in my search for tools, cobwebs,
five years old, looking for

the machines of life. The source
of life, I knew, as mysterious as
my mother's bedroom. I didn't touch
the egg for weeks, my brain resembling

its contours. Till the day came
I gave up waiting for the news, I
contrived to make it roll & fall
to the floor beside a rusted shovel.

Bending over, I knew first the
terrible stink, & then the quills
of light, bone, or fiber, it was
a wing never to be used. It's guilt

I carried for a year & then carried
lighter for more years, as if I
myself smelled, as if I had brought
those tender stinking wings to earth.

## The Beach at Veracruz

Your bare white legs
tight around the dolphin's back,

I see you dip below the wave
out of sight, to what world

of underwater castles, what
deep ride of deepening pressure
inside those thighs?

            The beach
at Veracruz, after nightfall, is not
Mexico of my mind. Loose

German sailors sit at booze tables
eyeing the girls of strange language

two by two, large tits into
the noisy dance places. Sweat rolls

between their legs in those
tight clothes, & the air is
too tight, not Mexico air.

Men with frowning faces search
everyone entering those places, running

hands along their legs, looking
for concealed guns, everyone

is too fat here, the American
gun boats sit like steel offshore,

the only birds are fugitive, streaking
along the edge of sand, wings
silent in the dark.

& I am silent, sitting
on the wet sand at night,

looking East, to sea, at moon
light slicing between the waves,

or it is the cool gleam
of your naked legs, hundred yards
out there. I havent seen you

for minutes, you have finally
found your sea away from every-
thing.

      I stand, as you descend, no
doubt about it, you hold that

dolphin tight, as you hold your
breath, as I hold my breath. I

yell triumphant as your moonlit face
rides a wave out of the night

toward me, & your moon, your
thighs move two & two toward me.


## My Atlas Poet

         threw a woman's shoe
    thru the mirror of memory

         and awaited seven years
   of bad luck
      when he married

            and became a poet
            eating and drinking
            on the rewards of it

Refusing ever to say "I" again
but always "we"
the world of women on his back

he planted seed in the Spring
and cultivated children
each one a superior poet
    at age two

All else washing out in pale paint
sketches of far countries
moulding in basement drawers

    all he felt
    was the muscle in his finger

    the strained tendons
    in his neck

Outside the world
and sustaining it
    where seven years is forever
        as seven minutes proved it to be


## Solid Mountain

Yes solid mountain mingle in my brain —
hear a mile of echo, it is my voice
calling out of my childhood, that is
important to anyone but my self?

I mark myself in the hilltop of your meat
I climb in my mind, your dark trees
in winds of my making,
how can I forget you, you are my past

that should be long forgotten, yes, drift
in the mountain winds, your name
soundless as the next valley's drift of snow
where my evening footprints are blue
as the creases in my brain lobes.

I cant forget, that's my problem, my
self interposes, it is a stranger
to my will, disruptive
meddler. I would say

forget him, forget him, but
will I remember that other, the person
I found on the foothills, coming down,
the other likelihood that I
suspect, I hope for, the
more memorable present, I recognize
as the person I can become
by forgetting? It is a woman

I watch on the street in this city,
myself flicking that skirt,
those boots, walking to the rhythm
of my own blood, carried down
the east slope of the mountain. I stay
my mouth from shouting hello it's me,
turn around & let us meet, me
& me, let us walk on the level.


## Smoking Drugs with Strangers

Smoking drugs with strangers
I slide between cities
with no distances.

We breathe one another
instead of the city air.

I encounter my own skin
on the arm of an ex-student in Detroit.

I sleep on a zebra skin couch
in the middle of my home town,
catching up on my alien childhood.

Smoking drugs with strangers
I drive my own car
over city streets uncreated
a moment before,
never getting lost,
the white line running down the middle of my frontal lobe.

I find women writing with my pen
moving my elbow
to their pictures.

I gander at all my old friends
sitting on the edge of my coffee cup
in a new kitchen across the border
I reach by puffing in an elevator.

Smoking drugs with strangers
is against the law.

Crime doesnt pay.
That suits me, I'll do it for free.


**Under**

Manhattan is no island, it
is streets. But the winter air
is cold ocean, air
from below the surface

the city makes steam of.
Walking those streets looking for
an eye that will look back
I shiver under my cape

knowing I can swim but not
knowing for how long.

## Grass, Grass

A clogged ashtray a dead lung,
old fish on a plate,
drear classrooms I enter & re-enter
saying next life I'll eat oranges every day —

. . . . . . . . . . . . . . . . . . . . . . . .

Let me speak to you
as before me I was spoken to:
remember to lie on the grass of cold morning,
not dreaming, but eyes open where they hurt
with the cold & the morning,
not commanding the sun,
not communing with the soil,
but wearing any shoes, any serviceable coat,
hands in pockets for the dew
of a finisht & unimportant night.

Then drive your car if you will
back onto the drying streets,
but merrily, merrily, & if you will,
remembering me, remembering that I spoke
even from collapsing lung,
even with raw-bitten fingers on your arm.

That I was allowed to say this,
that I intend to say it,
all the dew of morning remember, & the mist
that catches light before you see sun,
that is no longer night of unimportance,
that living fish are stirring in their water,
& dogs bark, seeing their breath,
& bark at their visible breath,
& that is to look at, smile or no,
that I
do not bark now,
I am not barking to no purpose,
I am not barking,
I am not a man barking.

As I am allowed to speak,
be there no morning, no walk.

I tell you as I was told,
you may even leave an orange outside the door overnight,
suitable to eat cold
even while you lie on the grass,
& its colour orange,
& its colour green.

# Aram Boyajian

**Poetry Is in the Darkness**

Poetry is in the darkness
under the silver and gold fillings
in the mouth of the chewer
under the tables in the brightest of rooms
knees being touched
in the bedrooms of couples
locked
under the lids of the sleeper
in his and her spaces between skin and bone
in the crevices of the brain
where everything falls in
in between legs that taste
of a billion years ago
the saltiness of amphibians at the edge
the wet dripping over the body
the body unstuck from the mud
and all the poetry stuck to the gut
— and a last glance back at the sea
full


**The World Is Really a Sugarplum House in the Forest**

The world is really a sugarplum house in the forest
We are all Hansel and Gretel diabetics
Too much    too rich    too sweet
Every room has every thing
and whole families curl up in their living rooms
and die together
Birds circle

eat the flesh
and vomit
In the heat and stench
I screw Gretel
and after an hour
still can't
The witch who owns the place
touches my penis
to see if I'm fat enough
I grow faint
and lose the use of my right leg
She gives me a lollipop and sucks me off
(a mixed metaphor)
She shows me a dirty picture
and I think of a woman
When I see a woman
I think of a dirty picture
The bitch witch
lifts her skirt
saying "stick your finger in"
I do
She says "Not enough
not fat enough"
Gradually we get used to each other
and one day I ask her
where the girl I came with
went
She says
"Stick your tongue in"
I do
She says "Not enough
not fat enough"
We have children
and I go to work
and come back at night
Sometimes I think of the girl I came with
She's a picture in my mind
I become depressed
and put a cold steel gun to my head
She says "Enough
That's just enough"

Wondering if I should think of her
as a picture of a picture
I pull the trigger
*Click*
I as dead
see everyone else as dead
there's that much selfishness
to the very end
She gets on me
and rides like the wind
She leans and wets my face
and spittles closed my already closed eyes
She whispers forever in the forever night
"The world is really a sugarplum house
But the forest — I sometimes wonder about the forest"

## George Washington Goes to a Girlie Movie

3 of Washingtons heads
fan and unfan
from my hand to his
The man who sells the ticket
tears the ticket
Silent pictures on the screen
with records playing
& 3 women on a bed
showing their all
Heads of middle aged men
who like me
when told in school
we would be the countrys leaders
didn't believe it
And now its all
come true
The 3 girls suck bananas
& wink their mascaraed eyes at me
I say to myself
barely moving my lips
"What am I doing here in the dark
a grown up man
watching 3 women

eat bananas"
That night
before going to sleep
my wife and I watch the news:
one Vietcong spy dead
shot in the head by a soldier
the reporter said
After watching this long enough
it gets very soft
and I start to swallow it
I say to myself
hardly moving my lips
what am I doing here in the dark
The night is especially slippery
what with my wife
and then me
and the 3 squirming girls
who were 3 girls on a screen
who are 3 girls somewheres tonight
probably having watched with me
that gun going off on the news
the gun which is now
a picture sound in my head
the gun at the side
of a sleeping soldier who
dreams of 3 girls giving him their all
on condition that he
1. shoot to kill forever
2. think of love forever
3. watch me watch them
eating bananas forever
That night I peel my penis
& the 3 women spit out banana mush
back onto the top of the banana
& the bullet cloud sucks back into the gun
& the dead man springs straight up
& the large missing piece of his head reappears
& he speaks that crazy sing-y poetry tongue of his
& I say to myself
hardly moving my lips
what am I doing here in the dark

37    *Aram Boyajian*

Drink fuck shoot up dope
take recorder lessons and a great book course
whatever you do
you will never be doing
what you are doing
I vomit up what was to have been
my flesh and blood
Bits of yesterday
come out of my mouth
& the 3 heads of George Washington
are deposited with a million heads of George Washington
one million heads with one million mouths
all saying to themselves together
hardly moving their lips
in a great incredible chorus
What are we doing here in the dark?


## American Commencement

1.

Out of every hundred of us
one hundred will go
to Dachau
Doctors will inject us
as experiment
We will touch wires and memory
equally dead
We will slide sexually into ovens
head first and bald
our hair clipped off
for beds in cat houses
Easy comes
Easy goes

2.

Out of every hundred of us
one hundred will go
to Hiroshima
We will speak perfect Japanese
and our bodies will blister
and run blood down
to the marrow bone
The Emperor on the radio is saying
the war is over
One Japanese skeleton with perfect round eye sockets
says to another Japanese skeleton with perfect round
      eye sockets
"Big fuckin' deal" —
only in Japanese it's
"Big luckin' leal"
It's true you know
what they say about Oriental women
:if you drop bombs on them
they die

3.

Out of every hundred of us
one hundred will go
to school and IndoChina


**Blok**
**Let Me Learn the Poem**

To Blok
words that had stuck together
like blood closing a wound
no longer did
At 41 he was through
He knew once
one Blok poem
could impregnate
an entire trainful of women

on the Moscow subway
during rush hour
Now he couldn't get through a turnstile
and go down the deepest escalator
in the world
He had gone
he said
to greater depths
but the engineers of steel and marble
didn't believe him
In his last years
Blok heard only the silences
of the trains that had gone
and the chug-a-lug
of the empty bottle
All his beautiful ladies left him
and became Christs
who never returned
ladies with beards
fondling themselves
in his dreams
tonguing the ecstasies
of themselves
Blok
let me learn the poem
and go down the escalator longer
than the longest in the world
to impregnate again the lady guards
and scrubbers down at midnight
who read your poetry surreptitiously
between the trains to come
and the trains gone
There
where no words are ever allowed
on the walls
let us scrawl them
poems that stick like blood
closing wounds

## The Death of the Epileptic Poet Yesenin

His flesh
fish underwater
clouds of sperm & eggs
the wonderful tumbling
head over heels of them
microscopically seen
millions of them
floating down
not ever knowing
it's mostly
towards death
*Snap!*
Yesenin hangs
and he turns
first the front
and then the back
When he stops
his nipples
are blue-black
Read him
& that blue-blackness
rubs off
It is in the blue cathedrals
& the lips of women
in the cold
He laughingly kisses them
with his gashed tongue
of poems


## The Hairs in My Nose

1

I think of God
as an old man with a white beard
sitting on a fluffy cloud
with a long finger pointing out of it
and creating on the 7th day
the hairs in my nose

2

I snip out the hairs in my nose
and from the drain it goes into a river
where fish go upstream to mate
and on the banks of the moon shiney river
rows of Chinamen sit sucking eggs
The sounds of egg sucking and thrashing fish
eggs softly sucked and thrashing fish
empty shells floating on the water and silence
& all because of the hairs in my nose

3

The real Homer was as blind
as the make-believe Homer
Whenever he met anyone
he immediately felt
for the hairs in their nose
"Stop!" cried a young ancient Greek lady
"you're pinching my cunt"
"O dear" said Homer
"and here I was thinking you had a terrible cold"
Watch out for poets
going through life
looking for the hairs in the nose

4

Jesus said "Where's the nearest delicatessen"
Then he wrapped his thick greasy Jewish lips
over the garlicky frankfurter
& took a swig of Dr Brown's Celery
He said "He who eats a frankfurter
& drinks Dr Brown's Celery
eats and drinks the hairs in my nose"

5

The ladies rolled back the rock
to see if the body of Jesus were there
They found no trace except
a memory of wings
and the hairs of his nose

6

In a roomful of the dead
— Jesus    Marilyn Monroe
Rimbaud    Harpo Marx
a clumsy dinosaur
et cetera et cetera
all had in common this
:infinity
& the hairs in their nose

7

Is God everywhere
The poet and the whore say yes to everything
even to a God who is
in the hairs of the nose

8

We went to an X-rated film
that showed in big close-up
all the hairs in the nose
When we came out
I said to my wife
"God I never imagined
they'd ever show such things
on the screen"
She agreed
That night
we kept all the lights on
& showed each other
each others
hairs in our nose

9

What is poetry
Why are there wars
Is there a God
Why are there hairs in the nose
Only the final question
answers all others

10

Instead of smoking cigarettes
I rolled & smoked instead
the hairs in my nose
After a week of this
my throat was lined with hairs
so much so
that when I ate
I laughed hysterically
"What's the matter with you"
my wife asked
I had to tell her
"This is the funniest
Manhattan clam chowder
I ever ate"
The psychiatrist in the nut house
they sent me to
spoke with the voice of the Captain
in the Katzenjammer Kids
"Eider yuz is crazy
or yuz been smokin'
the hairs in yur noz"

11

Such a beautiful day
& somewhere men are dying
Such a horrendous day
& somewhere men are making love
To the hairs in the nose
all days are alike
— except "today"

12

You may say
"hairs in the nose"
means something else
But I tell you
"hairs in the nose"
is symbolic for
hairs in the nose
There are such symbols still left
and they are the terrifying ones

# Harley Elliott

**After Picking Rosehips**

With every soft gush of my feet
walking in tall pasture grass
the rosehips at my belt rub together
an old rosebush song.

      The moon rings.   The clouds
are frozen full of geese

and I can feel the darkness
growing on my skin.
The world ends tonight

    It is so
beautiful    this time
I have decided
to move here forever.   Even after
reaching that yellow square of light
drinking soup
and going to bed
I am only another man there

lost in the covers and quilts.
    I am only dreaming
moving still in that space
of grass and goldenrod

a man with rosehips
walking in the speechless night.

## Brothers Together in Winter

We are squared off in the snow
a blue winter evening in Kansas
and he holds a whetstone in
his blue white fist.

Yes   we are going
to kill each other this time
once and for all.   It is about
something one of us
has or has not done.

On his forearm a murky bluebird
tattoo flies with blunted wings
between two veins. His body
seems to grow around it

and as his fist comes by
silent as a breath of snow just
missing my chin   we stop
frozen by the near connection.

Twelve years since that standoff
and still the moment
holds us
hard beneath the blurring moon.

We stand   his hand comes up
the stone glides by my chin.
Snow falls.

The bluebird
flutters outward
and our faces are like mirrors.

## Blessed and Resting Uncle

blessed and resting uncle
and your banjo
     hand flowered, ill played

     I would say it like that even now
an equation of sounds to say something other
     as it was when we put him there
     a general tearless day
typical with clouds, yellow grass
     some swallowing horsemen and wives

     dakota has no answers
for a man wasted on the banjo
          but rock
     self assured,
the granite fields with power not to suffer
     but allow
     holes opened in them
or at best a line of farmers
     in wide ties

kildeer were playing foolish at the grave
     that time
     pink boulders never covered well
the over ears norwegian haircut
     whiskey halitosis
or the way he stood at windows

     nictitating eyes
     like some hawk caught
in fingers of a foreign tree

## The Planting

Carrying a hammer on a quiet street
     one of those cheap kind   heavy
wooden handle   (I had already
looked forward and seen
     the head flying off at some
        important moment)
but it was tight then
     every edge

        crisp and dangerous

like an Indian ax found clean
and smooth in dirt

        a modern artifact
its points threaten within
the dangling paper bag

It is hot.
The birds scream as
childrens voices from the various lawns.
a dog eyes me
knowingly
        I could be the one
     the right intense moment reached
     on a summer street
the man who goes berserk in a great
        burst of surprise

     And like an echo I feel
the sense of a weapon condensing
     filling the metal it travels
up the handle   searching a place
     in my arm.

## On a Country Road

"shakin like the
leaves on the trees"
came out of my head
    once again
like a metal loop of tape
cutting thru the static

        Muddy Waters
        circa   1959

        recalling certain
unshakeable vignettes   at night
on a midwestern highway

her white pants

        shining
    mother of pearl
against dark legs
      and every other little
      thing inherent in
dark crossroads

(frogs along the US 81

    the radios hot
      misery

# The Natural Order of Things

The seagulls inland
drop to the hot black of kansas
    bright as bits of paper
scattering
        after the tractor.

I would see them far off

      a banner
    that follows the bent back
    of someone elses plow

    and recall once having
handled a shotgun here
      firing with no reason
    on no ones behalf.
The gull that was struck floated dead
        its wings
      locked outward
      like a wire
        suspended toy.

And now it happens
as I am plowing    It is always
within a separated landscape
    a white wheel of gulls above
            the sun
the red geometric tractor

crawling on a square of earth
         below

    turning alone at the
      end of the field
    beginning a new row.

## Crazy Horse Returns to South Dakota

No photographs exist.    This man
comes to us unrecorded

        yet recently
inhabiting the fitful dreams
of south dakota farmers.
They say he makes them nervous.    Watching
from a stand of cottonwoods
his eyes are like
two small dark moons

            regarding the various tractors
            that slice and rut the earth.

His horse is plain    he has
an average build    the most normal
of men    yet there is
a blue stone tied behind his ear
the sparrowhawk skin upon his head

and around his body a stormy light
        electric blue.

He appears suddenly
among the trees
as they are opening the earth

or just beyond their kitchen windows
still and watching

or seated on the ground
a hand upon each kneecap
        a pose adequate enough
for any man of beauty.

        And when the time comes
to describe his face
they stare into their coffee cups.

**The Panda**

*from*

**Animals That Stand in Dreams**

What can he want
appearing suddenly in my night life
    with those melancholy
    black stained eyes
    and shoe peg teeth?
War with China?
A misspent childhood?

The action goes on without him
as I ravage wet-mouthed starlets
and insult men twice my size
yet he remains
    seated in a corner of the dream
    like a forlorn trademark
    fumbling with a bamboo shoot.

It is only afterward
when I stand triumphant
and self-important over the
wrecked images
    that I turn to him

    and realize at last
that the face of my wife

when lost in her own dreams

assumes that same expression
which is at once
both comic
and full of unspeakable grief.

## Thinking Twice in the Laundromat

*1. Bird Dance*

Seeing you
in the laundromat
a beautiful African
form    certain and terse
as dark wood

I began my little
bird dance of hope
      afraid I may say something
      small town    and inane
                    like
        "welcome to america"

Your arm
loading clothes in an arc
      into the shining chrome circle
is alive

      as something that should
      point over plains
          (the other hand shading
               your eyes)
I am there
among mimosa trees

I release green birds toward you
I approach you
      and my arms are full of long
      rare feathers

I will buy you soap

      I will help you fold

your gleaming sheets.

## 2. Pink Blues

Shyly    after you left
coasting on the memory of your
deep skin
        I found the brown wool sock
        sprawled outside your dryer

In my hand

knowing the foot it holds
more than I should
        exploring him    (he is
solemn    he
wears glasses)

and remembering your pink lips

and my pink lips

perhaps it could be
someday    the way I'd like
seeing you in a supermarket
I would want
to say
        meet me in the laundromat
        I have your
        husbands sock
O la,    o    la.

# Doug Fetherling

**Dialogue 4 1 Voice Only**

*'the blues aint nothin but a good woman on ur mind'*
                    *Brownie McGhee*

the rain makes little cuts on the window
in the past 6 hours ive had 4 suicide attempts
        only 2 of them successful
the walls disappear then female fingers touching my cock
im interested in suicide as an art form

4 hour nitesleep in aeroport
almost got in streetfite w/ cleveland cop
i just about get used 2 1 country's cigarettes
        be4having 2 move
ive only seen those steve mcqueen movies lce

paranoia can be a way of life
i had 4gotten just how sexy american razor blades can be
she keeps saying, You remind me of
        my roommate's brother
i answer
        Dont breathe heavy less u really mean it

**Sex Play in Four Acts**

ive seen all the sunrises since u left me —
have spent 8 hrs w/ my boots in the aisle of all nite
cinemas horror four feature festival then stumbled
out horny on freshly watered yonge street fiting upstream,
the wind blowing back my corduroy coat lce worn by
        leroi jones

making bat wing type torn lining membranes between
my arms & sides, thru queer country music from
topless bars, fast past whole republics of porno
bookstores "includes never be4 publisht interview w/
actual lesbians", have run w/o ruth across to & up
university avenoo panting til my eyesve met headon w/
those of urine-soaked bone picker queens park 4.26
am sunday three inches away whereupon
ive cowered quickly under park bench to watch that
dawn w/o u &
                ull never take me alive

ours was the vietnam of love affairs —
i used to get stupid george to cover for me at
the newsroom so i could sneak out at midnite &
sleep til dawn w/ my nose in ur ear — i
told u about the french poets ud already read, u de-
clined my nouns w/ thanks — now on
queen street old men come to pawn their false teeth — i still
move my lips when i translate

unbelievably warm that december
we walked around the deserted park laffing
& falling after the ducks ... whod bean thru
it all so many times be4 — ur pubis whispered u
were a natural blond —
"ur god my god same god": old westerns too can get to
be a way of life — im thinking of having
a LOVE KILLS button made to hand out to
street sweepers who keep finding me asleep in alleys
amid overturned splintered vegetable crates no matter
how well i try to hide

yesterday i thot id die loving u
or (be loving u when i die)?

## She Employed the Familiar "Tu" Form

*("One employs the familiar 'tu' form when addressing pets,
small children or one's lover — but which was i?")*

hours after fate had brot us 2gether in
the public library — she had been just
standing there under maritime history, 910.4 in
the dewey decimal system — i brot her up
to my place for goats milk/
i just had turned my back for a second when
she took off her body & crawled under the covers:
like a chipmunk in bed: her small white hands
holding the sheets up over her breasts: the lites
from across the street throwing a big shadow
on her frenchjew nose against my wall/
her mouth did not speak english

i still can see her in her chemise in the morning @ the
top of the stairs as she was that day i went off to a
war — i 4get which one/ & whenever im in
my favorite montreal pub, the one with the
patron-saint-of-the-day on the blackboard so
u know who to toast, her voice calls to me
& i end up having to leave the radio on all nite
for fear of missing something

## Bathing with Father

Evolution, though a good thing, has
been carried to extremes. I began to
notice yesterday on the beach that I
have been evolving faster than the
others. The rest my age were all born
with useless appendices, of which
there's not been one in my family for
sixty years or more. And yet, for all
that, I am so different from my father.
I was born without pubic hair in
an age in which it didn't matter. And
father, I remember, had toenails, which
were useful during the Depression but
with which I wouldn't know what to do.
His skin was far more inflammable than
mine and seemed to be less impervious
to smog. And while there remains a
certain family resemblance I daily
grow more distant from the others on
the beach.

## Diseases of the Moon

I have had to stop answering yes and no
even to simple yes-or-no questions because
the way I live puts time in short supply
and I prefer to spend what little I have
pondering issues of inordinate complexity.

Two fairly typical examples of the recent
conclusions I have made are that the moon
is affected by the tides instead of the
other way around and that funerals ought
somehow to protest death rather than merely
acquiesce.

## Genius Loci of the Morning

I wake up first and with a sense of
tradition. You lie there still, your
knees drawn to your belly.
Hyperventilation is the word of the
hour. You are one massive lung
preoccupied with breathing while I
wander sleepily — a ghost making
breakfast.

The morning plays tricks with the
city beyond the window. Victorian
rooftops are again in the distance,
their turrets like nipples for the
feeding of afterdawn fog. Antennae
poke unpredictably skyward, clouds
put signatures to the stillness to
make it all official.

And now, both relieved and enlightened,
I rejoin you in bed ever so gently,
so that not even the cat, who sleeps
between our sets of feet, will be
disturbed.


## Your Absence Has Not Taught Me

Your absence has not taught me
how to be alone, it merely has
shown that when together we cast
a single shadow upon this wall.
The wall I suppose is as a wall
should be: plain and bare and
final as a cliff. And when I
stretch, my hand finds it instead
of you and I invent truths men
thought of years ago without
telling me.

## Shacked Up at the Ritz

Through our laced and latticed windows
all the sunlight of Montréal is aimed at
us who lie like two closed books enamoured
of each other's plots. Our view from
the bed is of mahogany and brass but our / eyes
stay focused on the tips of our noses.
The sun insists of covering us both
while your blood besmears the pristine
sheets like sacraments on a holiday.

## Nights Passed on Ward's Island, Toronto Harbour

*First night.*

The water like quartz, with the same kinds of strata,
briefly overhangs the shoreline before collapsing. Or
else, like an aeroplane disenchanted with flight,
flops in on its undercarriage to bury itself in the
sand. The regularity of small, freshwater waves is in
any case overrated.

This 'island' now is truly an island, as desolate as
the city across the way, more still than that skyline,
a parody of itself. But I sense the change around me
in an instant. The surf, if it can be called that, has
ceased its plunder and has turned instead to licking
the sand. The taste left in its mouth, the taste I
left behind me.

*Second night.*

The sound of hair against paper. Waking oval-eyed
in the near morning on newsprint spread on spongy
grass. The first ferry of the morning yet to come
Cottage screen doors bang in their frames. An image
put away for future reference. And my final cigarette
saved from extinction by a puff at the last possible
moment.

## Dispatch Number Nine

Women before were strangers,
no matter however friendly. My
knowledge of each would end
without a taper. Looking for
a face I would see only a
head, the features airbrushed
away like the private parts
of models shown in artists'
anatomy books. But with a
shift so slow and soothing
(like water running warm to
hot), that changed somehow in
Montréal, a city, it seems,
of dangerous joys.

## Dispatch Number Sixteen

The latest poems, like the most recent
women, were always the purest ones to
date. It had been that way forever
Till at some point really trivial — not
a climax or a milestone — you passed too
near a mirror and saw what you deserved,
an irrational facsimile of a very
desperate man
Who stood there, quite fastidiously,
with no one to be fastidious for, in
the centre of a room she's never been
in and which is made a hotel by her
very absence alone.

## Dispatch Number Sixty

Quitting is out of the question yet
remaining means a ghastly end: our
relationship is somewhat like a
shipboard fire in an icy ocean not
shown on any chart.

# Ray Fraser

**Flora**

The little girl I'd known
Grown up with sex on her mind
To fourteen years old, and blonde
By the field they burn every spring
To make the grass come green
And the smoke spreads over town
Like a burnt offering to spring,
She took it on her mind to undress for me
Like another offering to spring —
And this was what I dreamt last night.

**In an Empty Window**

I saw it in an empty window,
A life that's gone now.
It haunted me as a boy
And had the age been different
I might have been the young priest
The evening sun illusions in an empty
        window,
Staring out a gothic window
An organ playing through my soul
In the full empty church.
                I see
A shadow of it now, with my breviary
Across my breast, a young priest
In a world of black and white and doubts,
Long hours of twilight, soft voices,
Noiseless footsteps and long garments,

My solitary learning and evening walks
  by the trees,
Looking through a gothic window, and
  perhaps
Sweetly persecuting me a woman, fair
And soft, eyes flashing, devils in my
  heart,
And towering through the cathedral
The giant presence of a terrible God.


## Souster

I think it's worth it today
when I read Souster
although he's a mean little banker
and his wife isn't so beautiful
and he lives in a standard suburban home
in Toronto where
his years have been mostly routine
he hasn't made a million
or owned a yacht
or lived for years in Europe or the Far East
people who see him wouldn't know him
and to most his name wouldn't mean a thing
he can't lay an international whore
on the strength of his name
or the power of his bank account
he'll probably die the same way he's lived
with a small fame
and a smaller fortune
but when I read his poems
I think it's worth it
that a good poet's life
is well spent.

## Lost Picture

A young man of twenty
sets out to see his girl
on a wagon

he drives fifteen miles
with his hair combed
and his face shaved
a strong man
with fifty cents in his pocket

they go to the dance
the horse is tied in the stand outside
and the musical reel thrills their bodies
and riding to her home
on the wagon
they kiss and hold each other
and after there's the long ride home
alone in the moonlight
drunk with the memory of her
to the farm down the long dirt road
by the river


## On Learning to Play the Guitar

Having learned to play the guitar
now and I can accompany myself
to all the songs I've wanted to sing
I spend hours each day singing songs
and playing the guitar
and playing the part of the performer
which is a great pleasure to me
I don't write poems
because why should I write poems
when it's so much joy
singing the poems of others?
Beware, poets! of the guitar
lest you be seduced like myself

and become a happy minstrel
beware the loss of your misery
lest you lie dead in your grave
unaware that you spent your life
a happy nobody singing songs
rather than unaware
you left behind immortal lines
for other happy singers.


## Ecole St. Luc

A school that looks like an army barracks
that's a distressing sight
but the girls who go to the school
wear miniskirts
and that's not a distressing sight
and the boys have hair to their shoulders
and that's not a distressing sight
and the boys and girls sneak kisses
when the bell rings
and that's not a distressing sight
and the boys and girls light up smokes
as they mob out after school
and that's not a distressing sight
and the school is run by nuns
and that's an interesting thought
but it still looks like an army barracks
or an airforce hangar
and that's still a distressing sight


## The Cry of an Aged One

"Mr. Colwell"
says Sharon the nurse
"sits in his wheelchair all day long
and calls out:
come here!
come here!

come here!
an old man of 90
is Mr. Colwell
and all he says is:
come here!
and when a nurse
comes near
he touches her
and he's quiet
all he wants
is for someone
to hold his hand"


**The Grotto**

The maple buds were blossoming reddish tufts
the size of frilly little flowers this afternoon
I was over to the Grotto
There's a high barbed fence around it
but the gate was open
I used to play there when I was a kid
it's not kept in good repair these days
the floor is covered with broken bottles
and old leaves from last fall, bits of papers
some rusty bread pans (?), match cards, a chiclet package
but I didn't see any turds of shit
or french safes
so the fence has been successful to some extent
The grotto stands at the foot of a steep hill
in front of Mount Saint Joseph convent and home
     for the aged
it's made of porous stone and mortar
it looks like a chapel for little people
the doors and windows are so tiny
you have to stoop down to walk through
and your head hardly fits out the windows
but there's a big front door
that's open on the stone yard outside
where most people would have to worship if a mass
     were held

because the grotto inside could only hold a few
besides the priest and altarboys at the altar
The Grotto is roughly made with stones
hanging down from the ceiling like stalactites
and the walls are the same way
The door on the tabernacle is torn off
there is a pulpit overlooking the outside
which is reached by a winding stone stairway from within
bushes grow around the place
the grass was recently burnt
it looks like the hair on a bear
As kids we used to climb up on the Grotto's roof
it was easy climbing because of all the rocks sticking out
the roof is smooth in places
covered with mortar, but there are heaps of stone
that jut up like stalagmites
there used to be a statue of the Blessed Virgin
in the facade in front with a halo on her head
and a pipe running into the back of her head
which carried wires to light up the halo
maybe that's still there I didn't look
it wasn't a nice statue — kind of gaudy
colored blue and white
with a pipe stuck in its head
didn't belong in that rugged chapel
the high wire fence doesn't fit either
but it's probably necessary
to keep kids from shitting in the chapel
like they used to do

## Policemen Laughing

The two policemen laughed
but not with humor
at the big boots I was wearing
as I walked by them
presumably because the snow was all gone
and my boots scraped along the pavement
my boots were out of place
they threw back their heads
and pointed their fingers
and laughed ha ha.


## Not Often

Yesterday I stood on the balcony
of my girlfriend's apartment
on the fourth floor
at the back of the building
and looked at the windows across the yard

and in a window across the yard
as I stood on the balcony
a girl rose from her couch
and threw off her clothes
and stood in the window before me naked

even though she was big and fat
it hasn't happened often.

# Len Gasparini

**Niagara Falls Nocturne**

The same old souvenirs
still amuse us: pennants,
Indian wood carvings,
and the aphrodisiac cocktails
whose nectar we spill on pillows
like a newly wedded couple.

We spent our sleepless nights
rehearsing melodramas (I remember
your fondness for Chopin)
while the monotonous aquatic
thunder numbed our ears
and the braille of stars felt soft.

In a luxurious suite
overlooking
the picture postcard cataracts
we tickled the skin of dreams
and maneuvered our love
with hors d'oeuvres.

At night  the neon loins
of this city unveil brides galore.
O Rainbow Bridge!
believe me when I say
our honeymoon was nothing more
than breakfast in bed.

## Kafka's Other Metamorphosis

Franz Kafka had a nightmare
In which he, a butterfly brooch,
Was pinned between the limp breasts
Of a whore slurping cabbage soup.

He suddenly fell kerplunk
Into that bowl of sallow slime.
He did not drown — but emerged
As a magic caterpillar

And was swallowed on the spot.
The whore contracted syphilis
And had a chancre the size
Of a chrysalis on her crotch.


## The Accident

His finger resembled
A crimson asparagus tip.
I was with him.
I saw the accident.
It happened on the day shift.

An electrician was trying
To loosen a jammed V-belt,
Rotating the pulley
With his bare hand.    The motor
Was running but the V-belt wasn't.

I watched him intently, echoing
His curses.    It happened
So fast the sudden whir
Of the belt worried me.
He didn't cry out but shook

His bloody hand like crazy.
His right index finger
Was cut off below the knuckle.
Ugh! it looked horrible!
Somebody grabbed him before

He fell.   My stomach went weak.
They rushed him to a hospital.
I keep seeing his finger
In my sleep.   It resembles
a crimson asparagus tip.


## Valentine

A razorsharp wind
shaves the snowlathered
roofs of passing cars.

Holding my heart
in my gloved hands
I enter a barbershop.

The barber (whose frigid
wife I once seduced
on a bet) vengefully

slits my throat with
an icicle.   If you
visit his barbershop

you'll see a real valentine —
my heart in formaldehyde!


## Greasy Spoon Blues

Gus the Greek is a short-order cook
In a greasy spoon on Bloor Street.
He came here after their civil war
Thinking the streets were paved with gold.

After work Gus and I drink ouzo
In his furnished room, (if he's feeling
Good he'll play the bouzouki and sing
Bawdy Greek songs) then we top off

The night prowling pie-eyed in search
Of women horny as us.   "In Greece,"
Gus says, "there are many bordellos;
Here we put all our trust in banks."

And we ride the empty subway home
Cursing this country's affluence
That can't afford — or is afraid
To legalize whoredom and abortion.


## Written on a Paper Napkin

The snow falling outside
a restaurant window this morning
mocks my appetite
with each spoonful of cereal
I lift to my mouth.

Yesterday she undid
my ribboned bundle of love letters,
sneered *Such fine penmanship you have*
and tore them up one by one.
Mute, I watched her hands
make paper snow — the room cold.

*The snow falling outside*
*a restaurant window this morning . . .*

Yesterday I should have slapped
her face and said something cruelly
apropos; but the engagement ring
on her wormwhite finger
contained my hate in embryo.

# John Gill

**First Hymn**

*for A. M. Klein*

anything that promises    good
day    night    summertime    pregnant evil

do come    do come easier

the West brings storms and cutting wind
cables snapt and shingles blown

by South    the distant South    arrows
tipped dive into sun-beached haven

while North the big cream slowly spreads
white and blank    as mad as chaos

and Brother East yawns on his wide bed
promising what we know is foolish from heaven

so let's pray again and stamp our worship
onto stones and rings    let the earth smile

and let us rise like good bread
baked from sour mash    and wholesome leaven.

## As a Child Seeing a Cardinal

in the heat-locked room
a steamy view of snow
(huge fluffy clumps
sky of pearl grey)

suddenly a red-splash!

a CRESTED BOLD BIRD
rocking on a branch

and to my astonishment stays

on the roof of my mouth
and on my tongue
only redder much redder
and louder and longer

it stays like blood fact
like real life
like something that's cut out
and won't ever go away.


## Poem

something broke the dream
turned him over    the sun in his eye
to silence    a nearbye tree sighed
or was it a chorus of boys
shrill in the distance
"the eye, the eye, the honied eye!"

he was staring in the mirror
& from under his upper lid
a small moist stirring
then a grey moth appeared
small as a tear it squeezed out
& flew away    then 2 more insects came
one of them a sleek wasp
& finally 2 fat-bellied bees
pushed their heads & forelegs out
popping out before drawing back in

oh, the hidden pollen of his eye!
bees making him their hive
the others escaping
the taste of their possible honey
like ripe fruit bruised
his dreaming mouth.


**Late Spring**  *a heaving*
*a turning*

the swallows flap in waves against the house
they "chit-chit" nervously trying to nest
     under the roof of the porch
     in the rafters of the garage
     anyplace under the wide eaves
and the house rides high in the deep green sea
and robins row sporadically in the calm
and catbirds cry to their soulful mates
and the field sparrow sitting straight up on a spar
     singing land ho! on lookout
and dirty starlings prowl and poke beaks
     eyes gleaming for creamy eggs
and the yellow warbler in cheerful toil
     sweeps the deck of bugs and insects
he stares into the cabin where I sit and read
and meadowlarks, blackbirds, bobolinks spread
rising and falling to the horizon as the ocean heaves
while over us all our albatross the mighty hawk
stiffly circles and spirals catching the exhalations
of heat, cries, movement, sweat, turning them to account
as he glides, almost free, in his heaven above the waves
and we sail we sail rooted by his lightning
               sheathed and unsheathed.

## Before the Thaw

*(for Lyn)*

have you seen me   at all
riding country roads
right down the center

the blinding light from the snow
everywhere
going to milk barns to buy it raw

or looking out at the barns
from the "study" window
just waiting
for them to collapse forever

Indian ghosts underground
suburbs advancing in shock waves

the highway belting along from the city
taking that corner field of evergreens

the hawk reduced from the dead tree
by the pond

if so   you already know
what I mean about country pleasures
and are waiting   like me   for the thaw.

**"I don't hear any melody
breathing I hear."**

body full of bees
rising up & down . . . after
a long wash
    the ocean's endless shore sending back
    its thin retreating hiss   more & more

breathing I heard   then that full calm
& the doves rose from beside yr. bed
dovecote outside yr. window
    their low crackling wide-eyed interrogation stalking
    breath for breath   yr. breath   my breath   gone


## What Could Be

what could be sad sorrowful leaps of the imagination
rain falling in the garden   on the peonies
on the snowy green hydrangeas   what leaps!
and on the crisp tea roses
tiny fingerling leaps
a suave erasure of thunder   bumbling
swallows weaving low baskets of rain
the damp hearts of flowers opening
later
when it will be day or even the other
not to be mentioned   (night)
where leaps are   indeed   leaps

toads come out to hug the darker shadows
their soft sacs of skin
pulsing much faster than the night seems

cold rain in the garden and hot hot leaps
I am swimming in my mother's body
I leap   my father leaps
we leap again and again and again.

# Robert Hershon

## Kelly

I banked the five in the side,
missed the six, cried a little.
Kelly said when the legs turn to
jelly, cash it in.    He made the six,
blew the seven.    It's the legs, he said
you're dead when they go.    I pushed the seven in.
I don't care you're a doctor, a lawyer
or what, when the legs go, hang it up.
I missed the eight, him too.    I banged it in.
When mine go, they'll get me, he said.
I made the nine.    Kelly threw a dollar on the table.
He racked and I broke and I racked and he broke
and we played all night.

## The U.S. Coast and Geodetic Survey Ship Pioneer

I am so fragile this morning
I cannot last the day
I think it was the woman on the subway
the one with the spangled hat
who jostled me and broke
something loose inside
sending it careering through my body

From my office window
the Silvercup Bread sign across the river
comes and goes in the fog
The office manager has locked
the carbon paper in a closet
to guard against waste
I wish I could do the same

I heard last night that the Pioneer
mother and cradle to North Beach
was scrapped four years ago

Leaving from Frank's bar
Russ Morgan on the juke box
the slamming of dice cups
across the Bay Bridge
a voice in the back seat sobbing
I don't want to go I don't want to go
I didn't want to go on that fucking ship
I wasn't sailing    we drove on

It might be my pancreas roaming
stupidly wildly crowding my heart
my appendix    I haven't got an appendix
pounding at my armpit soon to burst through
"The office is our home away from home.
We should, and will, keep it as neat
as our own living rooms."

Woods and I in downtown Oakland
early in the bars in the morning
where the crew of the Pioneer
did not buy us anything to drink
and we certainly wanted something to drink
Woods was off the ship then
I of course never sailed
We drove back in the old Mercury
knowing we'd run out of gas on the bridge
but we drove on and we were cut off
at Gino & Carlo's and Parma's and the Bagel
Shop and Caruso's before noon

I think I have the mumps leprosy 24 hour plague
dying at sea    I heard they scrapped the Pioneer
but I never sailed on it      "All lights
must be turned out at the end of the business day."
My heart shines in the dark    Silvercup flashing red
white bread white bread white bread white bread
I'm driving on

## Spitting on Ira Rosenblatt

It was a great pleasure
spitting on Ira Rosenblatt
a fine forbidden thing
denied me by his mother
and my mother to ensure
that I would pass my Sundays
spitting on Ira Rosenblatt

He in the alley, I on the wall
spitting on Ira Rosenblatt's
hair and face and shoulders
each time he tried to escape
It was a grand thing to torment him
such a sweet and industrious pleasure
spitting on Ira Rosenblatt

Working up the spittle, a duty:
spitting on Ira Rosenblatt
I spit in the toilet these days
There is no one left to torment that way
not that willing and straightforward way
How pleasant Sundays were, high on a wall
spitting on Ira Rosenblatt


## Ireland Lake

a step on the path
makes the path new
a step off the path
makes a new path

blueberries
blueberries too
put your foot down
kill the grass

three of us walking
one far ahead
one far behind
i am useless

around the camp
they say
but valued for
my strong back

on the path
going to ireland lake
because we said
we were going there

above the treeline
hot and grey
the water thick
with orange bugs

we ate them
with brown rice
off tin plates
they had no taste

on the way back
down to the green
singing on the path
worth the burning

three of us walked
now one is dead
and one is troubled
i am useless

around the house
she says
but valued for
my strong back

on this path
this blueberry path
we are making
back from ireland lake


## The Swimming Lesson

shining children in the fog
cannot see their toes
deep down green
    they are told to let go
push against the sweating tile
push away
      I thought of that
but the dive into the cold
after the coldness of all year
the preoccupation with the blind
    this year
      the constant ear
against my stomach
the roaring this year
all sounds underwater
      the slow-motion leap
into the darkened stairwell
I have known such grace before
    regretting the fancied deaths
    of strangers
with stomachs of their own
waxy ears cold fingers
the first step was to say
    I am afraid
shining children in the fog
cannot see their toes
deep down green
    they are told to let go

## Four Translations from the English of Robert Hershon

### 1. Two Sculptors

Two sculptors
the lion of the moment
and his teacher
are cycling to the exhibit

But the young woman arrives first
With her hammer and knife
she defaces the statues

When the sculptors get there
they are surprised

### 2. Meeting a Friend

When I see a friend on the street
I come up on him from behind
strike him heavily on the shoulder
and shout YAAAAAAA!
This permits him time to consider
what he wishes to say to me

### 3. Smiling Baby

Will you drink some more
Smiling Baby Muscatel
Wine Drink?

Then perhaps
you will no longer be frightened
by your old shoes
in a corner of the kitchen
waiting
to be thrown away

*4. Red Cross*

But the Red Cross
came last night
and burned a doughnut
on my lawn


## A Boy Who Smells Like Cocoa

A boy who smells like cocoa
sits beside me on the train.
                It is too pat
that a boy the shade of cocoa
should smell like that, but sweet,
in the cold subway, the fat Brooklyn redheads
begrudging him his seat.
                He nods to sleep,
leaning against me, shuddering upright,
leaning again.   His mother,
across the aisle, stiffens, afraid
                I will push him away.
Wall Street.   Bowling Green.   Under the river.
Two women in hats compare their shopping trips.
Under the river.   When you talk on the subway
                You talk to everyone.
I got off at Borough Hall.   The boy slept.
I never saw his eyes.
                A very old messenger
took my seat.

# Geof Hewitt

## Behind That Wall My Roommate Fucks His Girl

I could have said makes love
but only I do that, others fuck or screw
I scowl in my corner and turn the hi fi off
to hear them better: oh tasting love
through the ears is such a painful thing:

my parts numb as my ears stand up
attentive as trees: they are in that room
forever, bouncing gut to gut, flesh slapping
on the squeaky bed. And in my mind all the beds
I ever squeaked in, all the rooms I'd wished
I'd been in, float like pure heaven, serene
and easy, quiet in the night, disturbing no one.


## Emergency at 8

Across the street, my aunt has lost
      her baby: for nearly as long
      as I can think back, we've had to be so
Careful with her: no games at all
      for one thing and brush by her
      in tight corners without even touching
That wall of stomach, breakable as some new egg.

But now the sirens have died in my ears
      like adult voices, come and gone
      and taken her: she'll have to stay
Away awhile, getting better
      and forgetting all the work she wasted:
      holding eight months my broken cousin.
My house is quiet at this time. My mother holds the phone.

## Conversion

My hands have developed eyes!
I put them around corners
And under ladies' skirts: each
Finger blinks its joy to me:
My nose awakens in delight:

My tactile nerves exist at the ends
Of other things: the hymnal that girl
Holds against her breast has my
Neurons: Her stockings are the tips
Of my fingers. I ride between her knees.

My tongue is everywhere. It hastens
To a place before I know I want
A taste: I like my tongue. It rolls
The words of total strangers to new,
Unprecedented thoughts. Priests cursing

At the Mass, a Congregation stunned:
Some girl with me between her knees caught
Midway in surprise; she genuflects.
The eyes that were my fingers seeing
And caressing church tight breasts.


## For Randie

What college kids we've grown up
into — looking for a road to get
lost on, any place without a street lamp,
dark enough to let my fingers prowl.

How carefully I try to wrap you in a dream
that tells you I am safe, a lover
you can take for just a little while:
I'm dirty and new in town and guaranteed

to leave before your Wednesday paper.
And so we weave back to your room
between the white, insistent dorms,
past your mother-of-the-house,

beyond the voice and eye and knowledge
of your teacher, who is my friend:
The cockeyed gateman wants to let me know
he's been there too.

## Explanation

for Mike

I say the women don't sleep right
here in Iowa:
                their heads
balance badly
on my arm,
their thighs put me to sleep
waist up. Dreams jerk
them long after I'm ready for sleep,
their real loves waiting,
indifferent, in far off towns.

## Rip-off #1: Hippie Capitalism

fill your dark glasses with water & toast
the soggy success of American prisoners;
not even the cops are happy!

the kids have rolled a joint big as Baltimore
there's a bite in the cake for everyone
but who will eat cake

when there's pork on the fire?
We're on the corporation chart
we're part of the plan.

ta-ta, pigeye.

**For Bill**

*"Insomnia is only lack of trust in time."*

& when you try to sleep
the dream of dreaming shakes you

back: but you keep blinking at the dark,
you might be an owl

& practice wisdom.
Or a nightcrawler

through which time moves.
Difference between earth

& wormshit
is the time it takes a worm

to move the distance
of his length.

So don't be short, Bill,
just because you haven't got much sleep.

# Emmett Jarrett

**For E. C. J.**

You could smell the river
from the front gallery
on spring evenings, and hear
bullfrogs croaking in the shallows
across the levee. Moths fluttered
about the yellow porch light.
We sat in the swing
and rocked gently back and forth
as the creaking chains
back and forth kept time.

You told me Bible stories:
of David and Jonathan
and the young Moses
sorely tried with temptations,
of Samuel the priest
who heard God calling him.

We listened closely
as the darkness slowly
settled down on us
and closed us in on the gallery,
to the song of the quail
on the other side of the levee
and its repeated answer.

Bob white!
                    The answer:
Peas ripe!

(Straining to see, to hear!)

Bob white!     Peas ripe!

**Song**

*for Annie*

Help me now.
She is like a little child,
loves me the way
I always wanted to be,
and now I've got it
she is like a little child.

There are strings:
she is like a little child
who pulls her dolls apart,
wants them back again.
I pull the strings: because
she is like a little child.

I don't dare let go:
she's tangled me
in nets of my own making.
Dark pools.
A single silver fish gives light
and she is like a little child.
Help me    now!


**"Hamlet"**

I'm having an affair with Hamlet.
Every day I sit in my room in rue Monsieur le Prince &
    pound away
        at the typewriter trying to pluck out the heart of
            his mystery
        for seven hundred & fifty dollars,
then every night I go out & walk along the Seine,
    howling quietly
        to the moon,
& end up always alone on the Vert Galant:
he's there hiding behind a tree, waiting for me.

91    *Emmett Jarrett*

Underneath a concrete park bench we wriggle out of
    our clothes like
        snakes & start to make love immediately.
We suit one another perfectly.
I've got an educated cock, I twist it and turn it
    deliciously in his
        asshole & his mouth,
& when we suck each other off our tongues play around
    the hard rim
        of the head of our penises like warm rain in July.
We're not like the Egyptians on the Right Bank,
    who'd rather be
        clean than comely:
we're both of us uncircumcised, Herodotus.

O we're beautiful, our bodies are beautiful & our souls
    are beautiful,
        our teeth & eyes & hands, our sacred hearts
            are beautiful,
the green willows hanging in the park are beautiful,
the moon above Paris is beautiful, & the music of hundreds
    of French beatniks,
who crowd the Vert Galant right down to the edges of
    the quais,
they are all beautiful too.


**Human Relations**

Terry is sitting in the kafeneion writing letters to all
    his friends
asking for money. If everyone sends him what he asks for
he'll have two thousand dollars. A rich man in imagination,
he hasn't the money to pay for his mikro kafe
so he must sit and drink more and more coffee till he hates it,
waiting for me to come back and pick up the tab.
He secretly hates Annie for throwing him out in the cold
but he doesn't dare tell me because I might not pay
    for his coffee.

Annie is sitting at home in front of the little electric heater
hating the Mediterranean weather for being cold and damp.
She had a right to expect the sun to cooperate, she thinks,
with her image of Mediterranean weather.
Annie hates Terry the more because she threw him out
        in the cold,
which was illogical in the first place, neither her fault
        nor his.
I am the key to the whole situation,
a classic triangle, classically screwed up.
I invited Terry in the first place and Annie resents it.
I let her throw him out in the second place so Terry
        resents it.
And I pay for his coffee at the kafeneion every day.
Terry resents his dependence, and Annie,
who counts the drachmas in my pants pocket every night
after I'm asleep, resents every last drachma.

And here I am in the middle of nowhere
stranded in a broken down Greek bus.
The gears won't mesh. I'm late for work
but not disturbed in the slightest.
The driver has just picked up a large rock.
He is debating whether to bash in the motor
which he resents because it won't work,
or bash in my head because I sit here so calmly in the crisis
writing in my notebook in a strange language
while everyone else shouts helpfully to the gears to shift.


**Dear Mother**

thank you for your recent letter
I'm glad you liked the book of poems I sent
in spite of the fact that one had sex in it
I'm writing a new book now
with a poem in it that talks about homo-
sexual sex    you won't like that one either

I'm sorry to hear you don't like long hair
and beards    my hair is down to my shoulders now
and often dirty    even though I bathe twice
a month    like you always told me
my beard is long and stringy    like Fu Manchu
or maybe Ho Chi Minh    you
might call it kinky    I'll send you a photo
in my next letter    you can put it
on the mantel over your fake fireplace
next to the one of me in Army uniform

You'll be happy to know that my wife
still believes in the sanctity of marriage
she's assigned me a penance of $5000
in return for a divorce    I hear from your
neighbors that Uncle DeWitt died    and left you
a legacy    you never liked DeWitt
and neither did I    how about giving me
half of it    for my divorce

and by the way    the reason you keep
getting letters from Columbia asking
my whereabouts    is that I owe them money
why don't you write them a note    saying
"i regret to inform you that my late son
died early this morning    of syphilitic paresis
of the brain    which was communicated to him
by that damned Yankee Jew girl he's been
going around with    i'm just a poor widow-
schoolteacher    trying to make ends meet
don't bother me about that good-for-nothing's
debts    he's just like his father"


**The Trip**

I carry three passengers on a nightly journey:
a reluctant taxi driver, I take them always
farther than I want to go. Two women:
one who will not let go of me, the other
will neither take hold of nor follow me.

I don't know who the man is.
If we come to a fork in the road
perhaps he will take one of the women
away in an airplane or boat. Or maybe
we'll leave them both and exchange identities.
The worst would be to remain as we are,
unwilling companions, driving around forever.
Already the meter has ticked up an astronomical fare.


## The Two of Cups

*for Carol*

A burst of steam from the pipes in the morning startles me
when Jehovah's Witnesses knock on the door I turn
        them away
I would like to be kind to them but my mind's distracted
friends have begun to avoid me because I talk incessantly
        of you
they know you themselves and think there is no need
        for talking
then I sit morose and silent    abstracted    looking
        at the clock

the wind blows up a little whirl of snow in the parking lot
and I see you in pink and blue skiing down a steep slope
with one graceful motion you turn and stop just above me
a quizzical smile is on your face    then you are gone
I sit by the phone and wait for you to call
when it rings I spill coffee on my pants rushing to answer it
afraid if I say too much you'll hang up

I go to the Metropolitan to see the New York Painting show
as I wander through galleries Pollack seems tame
Arshile Gorky's furious images of sexuality are colorless
compared with any night last week with you in our bed
or the time we broke the bed in Stanley's house

I read the Tarot cards:    strife is over but a death is coming
my self is the woman walking through swords but my house
      is the house of the Fool
the outcome is the Two of Cups, the lesser lovers
Let the part that must die die quickly    come to me, love
walking over that reeking corpse with gingerly step
exchange cups with me    it's almost St. Valentine's Day
the Greater Lovers hover protectively over our heads
      in the morning

# George Jonas

**To Christian Montpelier**
*from*

**IV**

A single naked wire at ground level
From one end of the world to the other
Across the diamond-white, frost-bitten night,
Six yards from the ditch where our corpses would fall,
One mile from a highway, six miles from a town,
Sixty-two miles from the street where I was born,
Just a glance away from the brilliant moon,
A well-engineered, silent, seven-pound land mine.
It may not have seen me, I have seen it in time,
Now I can mention it briefly in a poem.


**Peace**

I wish to make a positive statement
Of happy hunters returning from the woods.
Wardens of dwindling flocks, serious concern
Dwells in their moist and beautiful eyes.

There is no conflict that love or bullets
Could not resolve in time.
Gardens are carefully planned. Long rows of roses sit
In all directions around any house.

There is always a period of peace
Between two blows, when a smiling landscape
Surrounds with blue light the resting warrior.
The raised arm hardly shows among the ferns.

At such times rabbits jump out of their trenches
And stand listening at the entrance of the field.
Worms pop out of the ground in open amazement,
Sharp-beaked birds freeze unfalling in their dive.

The moment is guarded by dustbins along the streets
Of low and crippled suburbs where later
Children come out of hiding and women pause for breath.
Hate, suspended, sways gently back and forth.

Rats are pacing the floor, thinking,
A loaf of bread cuts itself into warm slices,
A glass of milk travels to India,
Warships lean on their guns and close their eyes.

The beauty of such moments is hardly useful
Except for the purpose of missing a heartbeat,
As old men sit at tables, ready to talk.
For there is nothing to talk about.


**Once More**

Kirov was shot, Solon will rot in jail,
even the smallest hold-up man will hang,
Eichmann has died seven times, but the real,
the real murderers all live in my street.

They go to work each day at eight o'clock.
Some take the bus, some drive, and many walk.
They have a child or two, they like a smoke,
their wives wear rings, Sunday they cut the grass.

They talk about the business, the weather,
there is a faint click as they lock the door.
Only a few of them would hurt a fly
and all of them support a family.

Will they be caught? Is theirs the perfect crime?
All I see is the circle of the time,
all I know is I have to be prepared.

Caution causes me to glide through the walls
at night and stand beside them just to see
how long they have to wash their hands before
they turn the light out and they go to sleep.


**Portrait: The Freedom Fighter**

In the streetcar conductor's uniform
The man tried to roll himself a cigarette
Without letting go of his machine gun.
"It's a dog's life," he said, scratching himself
        with satisfaction,
"Rotten war," he said, viewing with deliberate pleasure
The hulk of a burned-out streetcar among the
        torn cobblestones,
"Want a fag, kid?" he asked me, being an elder
For the first time in his life among his passengers.
Later the night came but he did not go to sleep
In the cool mist and total darkness the city belonged to him
"It will be a long time before we mop up the bastards,"
And he waited for approval and reassurance.
The barricades ran half way across the square,
When he turned his eyes toward me I hesitated to answer,
He looked at my face but he was looking at my skull.


**Exit Lines**

At present I still have
A choice of deaths,
I could, for example, die of a difficult disease
For medical science and I could
Die for a stranger who has never learned to swim.
I could also die for the Queen.
These are quite honourable deaths
But they don't appeal to me.
I think I'll die for Barbara.
Strangers are strangers
Whether they can swim or not
Barbara is a friend.

Medical science
Requires long hours, depressing nights
In hospitals, syringes and white towels
For Barbara I could die with my clothes on.
The Queen, lovely as she is,
Has no breasts to compare with Barbara's
And I have never kissed the Queen's throat.
It makes sense for me to die for Barbara.


## Eight Lines for a Script Girl

I almost know you now. You are your name,
The substance of your skin, the movement of your eyes,
The line of your lips, the texture of your hair,
Your phone number, the colour of your voice.

You are your breasts' shape, the full length of your limbs,
You are your smile, your nailpolish, your dress.
Later I'll know you more. Still later
I'll know you even less.


## Four Untitled Poems

**1**

Women don't travel in clubcars
Young and innocent women especially don't
Salesmen travel in clubcars
And junior executives who don't rate airplane tickets
And senior executives who do but have heart conditions
So the girl in this clubcar is sitting pretty
The conductor gives her his full attention
Causes a little table to be lowered beside her
And personally tenders her a glass of tomato juice
And stands by until the rim of the glass
Has safely found its way to her suspicious lips.
Meanwhile the train moves onward to Montreal
Ancient forests yield to its passing
One can hear the wheels whispering to the axles
Did you know we have a virgin in the clubcar?

Soon she will respond to the last call for lunch
A happy piece of salmon will sit in her plate
Which she may reward with half a gentle smile.


**2**

Let me put it this way:

If I were a German
I could say to myself Mozart & Rilke
But I would also have to say
Goebbels & Bergen-Belsen
Words I could not pronounce lightly.

If I were a Frenchman
I could say Molière & Camus
But I would also have to add
Napoleon & Petain & The Maginot Line
In an embarrassing footnote.

As a Belgian I would have to reconcile
Verhaeren with the Congo
And as an Englishman subtract
The Boer War & The Playing Fields of Eton
From Milton & Yeats
Which may leave me with very little.

As a Russian I'd have to work hard
Fixing my thoughts rigidly on Tolstoy
And trying to forget all about Djerzhinsky,
And if I had to call the U.S. of A. my home
It might be more than my selective memory could handle.

But being a Canadian
By conscious and considered choice
I have to remember no one & nothing
Which in this 1969th year of grace
Suits me just fine.

**3**

      We all have
A bench in the park to reach
And some of us reach it.
I saw an old man this morning who did.
He seemed to be happy.

Green, black and brown were the predominant colours,
The sky threw in some blue, the clouds some white.
He himself was pink.

He held a stick in his hand, a safeguard of some sort
Against gravity, dogs, the universe,
The dangers of existence, his own buckling knees,
All known enemies inside and outside,
Even perhaps the Angel of Death.

Well, a stick is better than nothing.
He must have been eighty, he must have known
All fights are unequal
Otherwise how could there be victors?

Sitting among modest flowers
A kind of victor himself
He raised his eyes to follow my progress.

**4**

Sleep only with strangers
    for strangers sleep in peace
And will be perfect hosts
    you being a perfect guest
May touch nothing of yours
    and you nothing of theirs
Except their outer skin
    And the coffee-pot in the morning.

Sleep only with strangers
    for they are open and kind
They know you are here today
    and gone tomorrow
If you carry away a little object
    they can spare it
If you leave one behind
    they can throw it out the next day.

Be a knock on the door
    a voice on the telephone
The promise of a postcard
    without a return address
Sleep only with strangers
    it is for you they reserve
Their freshest linen
    and their cleanest smile.

## The Glass Eaters

There are half-naked men who stand
In the full heat of the sun.
I am told they chew on bits of glass
And swallow them one by one.

They scoop the glass up in their hands
Then pulp it with their teeth
And although they gulp it down carefully
Some are greviously cut.

In fact, the lips of some are said
To be a single gaping wound,
Their tongue only a piece of flesh,
Their gullet a mass of blood.

They must have a reason but to most they look
Like any group of men
Who stand half-naked and chew on bits of glass
In the full heat of the sun.

# Etheridge Knight

## Apology for Apostasy?

Soft songs, like birds, die in poison air
So my song cannot now be candy.
Anger rots the oak and elm; roses are rare,
Seldom seen through blind despair.

And my murmur cannot be heard
Above the din and damn. The night is full
Of buggers and bastards; no moon or stars
Light the sky. And my candy is deferred

Till peacetime, when my voice shall be light,
Like down, lilting in the air; then shall I
Sing of beaches, white in the magic sun,
And of moons and maidens at midnight.

## Haiku

1

Eastern guard tower
glints in sunset; convicts rest
like lizards on rocks.

2

The piano man
is sting at 3 am
his songs drop like plum.

3

Morning sun slants cell.
Drunks stagger like cripple flies
On Jailhouse floor.

4

To write a blues song
is to regiment riots
and pluck gems from graves.

5

A bare pecan tree
slips a pencil shadow down
a moonlit snow slope.

6

The falling snow flakes
Can not blunt the hard aches nor
Match the steel stillness.

7

Under moon shadows
A tall boy flashes knife and
Slices star bright ice.

8

In the August grass
Struck by the last rays of sun
The cracked teacup screams.

9

Making jazz swing in
Seventeen syllables AIN'T
No square poet's job.

## The Sun Came

*And if sun comes*
*How shall we greet him?*
    *Gwendolyn Brooks*

The Sun came, Miss Brooks, —
After all the night years.
He came spitting fire from his lips.
And we flipped — We goofed the whole thing.
It looks like our ears were not equipped
For the fierce hammering.

And now the Sun has gone, has bled red,
Weeping behind the hills.
Again the night year shadows form.
But beneath the placid faces a storm rages.
The rays of Red have pierced the deep, have struck
The core.   We cannot sleep.
The shadows sing: Malcolm, Malcolm, Malcolm.
The darkness ain't like before.

The Sun came, Miss Brooks.
And we goofed the whole thing.
I think.
(Though ain't no vision visited my cell).


## To the Man Who Sidled Up to Me and Asked: "How Long You in fer, Buddy?"

You need lightning
to strike the circle of the moon
your teeth    false
click nicely

and
you are
acey deucey tight

yours is the song
of massa
        so kissed
jest looking fer a home
jesus looking for a home

you need lightning
to strike the circle of the moon
your eyes
sing
empty psalms


**For Freckle-faced Gerald**

Now you take ol Rufus. He beat drums,
was free and funky under the arms,
fucked white girls, jumped off a bridge
(and thought nothing of the sacrilege),
he copped out — and he was over twenty-one.

Take Gerald. Sixteen years hadn't even done
a good job on his voice. He didn't even know
how to talk tough, or how to hide the glow
of life before he was thrown in as "pigmeat"
for the buzzards to eat.

Gerald, who had no memory or hope of copper hot lips —
of firm upthrusting thighs
to reenforce his flow,
let tall walls and buzzards change the course
of his river from south to north.

(No safety in number like back on the block.
two's aplenty. three? definitely not.
four? "you're all muslims."
five? "you were planning a race riot."
plus, Gerald could never quite win
with his precise speech and innocent grin
the trust and fists of the young black cats.)

Gerald, sun-kissed ten thousand times on the nose
and cheeks, didn't stand a chance,
didn't even know that the loss of his balls
had been plotted years in advance
by wiser and bigger buzzards than those
who now hover above his track
and at night light upon his back.


## For Dan Berrigan

I don't know about you, whiteman all dressed in black
I mean I really don't know just where you at
Maybe your far ahead of us or far behind
Maybe you see it all, whiteman, or maybe you blind.


## Upon Your Leaving

*for Sonia*

Night
and in the warm blackness
your woman smell filled the room
as our rivers flowed together, became one
in love's patterns, our sweat / drenched bellies
made flat cracks as they kissed
like sea waves lapping against the shore
rocks rising and rolling and sliding back.
And
your sighs softly calling my name
became love song's child / woman songs
old as a thousand years new as the few
smiles you released like sacred doves. and I
fell asleep, ashamed of my glow, of my halo, and
ignoring them who waited below
to take you away when the sun rose. . . .
Day
and the sunlight playing in the green leaves
above us fell across your face traced the tears
in your eyes and love patterns in the wet grass.

and as they waited inside in triumphant patience
to take you away I begged you to stay.
"but, etheridge," you said, "i don't know what to do."
and the love patterns shifted and shimmered in your eyes.
And
after they had taken you and gone, the day
turned stark white. bleak. barren like
the nordic landscape. I turned and entered
into the empty house and fell on the floor.
laughing. trying to fill the spaces your love had left.
knowing that we would not remain apart long.
our rivers had flowed together.
we are one.
and are strong.

# Tom Kryss

**Breaking Ground in Me**

Have learned to burn my hands with fire
and to think of myself as a sort of backward
government with various seats of power
struggling to dominate each other.
Ignorance is my most important product
so that the peasant with the ploughshare
is a greater asset in this life
than the governments which rise
and fall.
His horse-like obstinacy
and deference to being seen
as a force running counter
to the landscape, in other words
his supreme talent for becoming the
earth he farms,
is the gravity which keeps
the atmosphere from drifting
into space.
He can usually be trusted
to throw another log on the fire
when the game grows exceedingly dark
and I put my brains on the table
and wish my eyes away,
wish I could unlearn my hands
and all the sensations
which run through them like chains.
The peasant says everything is fine:
"You don't need a weathervane
to know which way the wind
blows."

(The peasant is something
    of a singing clown also.)
Sometimes
I feel like Spring
in a country right after
a civil war.
No one is farming
where have the birds gone
why are the waters black
no one is watching
the hare running through me
out through the end of a log
and into the sky.

## And Jesus Don't Have Much Use for His Old Suitcase Anymore

Wherever the dark cloud horses galloped
the grass stretched its small fingers after them
and died
whole streets blew down and away like newspapers
a man walked into a barbershop
claiming he killed Ezra Pound
and shipped back the body in a trunk that smelled
of 98-proof manuscripts
He cried in Italian GOD WHAT HAVE I DONE
WHAT
HAVE I DONE
GOD
            and walked right out
The barber still slept in the chair
with a magazine on his face.
Another man came out of Texas, walking
with white hair and blue eyes blowing
swearing and raising all dust and hell
over the abandoned pickup trucks he found
he couldn't get over it
this huge music caught in the trees
like empty parachutes
these ballads
without men.

## Nothing Strange

at the end of the day
the machines have been silenced
our ears are large as empty boilers from which
the steam has passed, and the mice come out
of their holes to stare at the shadows
which we leave on the floor

we walk out into the light
and when my eyes hit the street there
is a shaking in the air, something
that recognizes me and wants
to run into my arms

but my arms are at my side
and the children look through me
as if over my shoulder
the sun is setting

passing the drugstore
i see the small water toys in
the window that have
their own peculiar light of things
that have not changed positions
for a winter and a summer

my hands go instinctively
to my pockets and i stand there
in my heavy shoes like a man
at a strange grave
watching the grass that
has grown.

## This Wind

this wind
i cannot place my fingers on
it is the wind
that crushes small animals
to the floor of the forest
that
blows down silos across the highway
it is nine minds high
and gathers in election squares of the world
it comes when the plastic radio
melts in my hands on the eve of the revolution
while i lie in bed smoking
Turkish cigarettes
it is populated by numbers
that predict the outcome of more numbers
which click against each other
like pelvic dice
this wind that wanders through the capitals
and assassinates the wrong dictators in their pajamas
this wind with the Winged Victory's arms
lodged in its throat
in its ionosphere
minoan prayer rugs sailing on
currents of yellow nitrogen
this wind
that dashes grains of sand like needles
against The Electric Curtain and scratches
Mayan rubrics in the glass-eye of Radio Free
David Sarnoff
this wind is the loneliness of the mob
it is a tree of wind bent into the moon
it is bounded on all sides by the echoes of stars
it is the gentle wind that cleans the spiders from my eyelids
it is the wind that carries Caesars to my door
i turn them away into the night with their speeches
        in their hats
and i listen to their footsteps in the wind / the wind
that only dead men do not hear.

## Bell Too Heavy to Ring

Words are sardines packed
in a man's eyes
some say they are still used
like the boulder money
of the Easter Islanders
carried from place to place
on sagging poles,
that they are no more permanent
than the buildings
after the air raids on London
in which some men managed to live
and some died
or bits of pottery in the earth
on the outskirts of a city
where people once camped,
pointing out that the viaducts
of Rome are now roads
hostile with flies and
human garbage.
A few have believed that
the language could be fashioned
like an arrowhead
or grafted onto old skin,
yet others seemed to know that
words were a petrified forest
dense and nerveless
dangerous
to traverse the forest
of heavy trees that either
turned back the sun
or let it struggle through chinks
and fissures,
places called days.
The poetry of children
who wrote in German death
camps, is said to be
magic
an affair of black atoms
and sunlight

foaming together,
a piece of barbed wire
wrapped around the night,
seagulls running on a beach.
One man took
all the magnums and cannon of a war
and melted them down into a bell
too heavy to ring.

## A Suicide

I moved to the window to wait for somebody
to come around.
There was nothing to do.
It was a few minutes past noon,
and the postman was walking away down the drive.

He left two letters.
I returned to the bedroom.
The body was stretched out on the bed,
I looked at it.
It used to belong to me.

I tried to kick the gun under the bed,
but I could not find my foot.
Then I tried to light a cigaret,
but my hand was not there.
It was hanging over the edge of the bed.

This is not so good, I thought,
and already I was beginning to wonder
Is there a way to get back in?
Is there a gun that will
blow your brains back in?

I had forgotten to empty the ashtrays
and pull the curtains.
Now somebody else would have to do it.
For an hour nobody came.
Then I saw a strange woman coming up the sidewalk

to the house.
She turned the door knob,
and came right in.
She called my name.
I didn't recognize her.
She left my mail on the table,
then she walked around the house,
pulling all the shades and emptying the ashtrays,
and I followed her.
She went into the bedroom.

Now I thought that she was going to throw
up her hands and scream, but no,
she merely looked at the bed,
and started to make it.
It was the normal thing to do.
She pulled the sheets over the body,
and tucked them in all around.
Then she straightened her skirt,
patted her ass,
and went into the kitchen.

The sink was filled with dishes.
She washed them.
Hanging on the wall was a painting
of the Last Supper.
She straightened the painting.
She opened the window to let some air in,
flipped on the radio,
and started to polish my shoes.

The doorbell rang, she answered it,
and came back with a man.
I didn't recognize him either.
They sat at the table,
talking about things,
but I did not learn too much from the
conversation.
Mostly, they talked about their friends,
who I did not know.

Pretty soon they went into the bedroom.
I did not follow them.
I heard a loud thud on the floor,
and much heavy breathing.
Then I heard nothing because they
closed the door.
I tried walking through the door,
but I could not do it.

About twenty minutes later they came out
of the bedroom.
The man was carrying his shoes,
and the woman had on a pink slip.
They were talking about how good it had been.
The man put on his shoes,
and the woman walked him to the door.

The woman stood a long time at the window,
looking out at the street.
The sunlight shone on her bare shoulders.
She put her hands on her shoulders,
and shivered.
I moved up behind her,
and put my hands around her shoulders,
but it occurred to me that
I did not have hands anymore.

She turned around and faced me.
Her face was blank.
Her fingers were playing with
the small silk flower at her neckline.

I was not sure who she was,
but I was beginning to feel that perhaps
I had known her not too many hours ago.

I followed her back into the bedroom.
The body was gone.
The bedsheets had been undone.
I saw that there was clothing on the floor,
and under the clothing I could make out

the gun.
She walked over the clothing,
and threw herself on the bed.
I could not see her face.
She was holding the pillow to her face.

I returned to the window,
and waited for somebody to come around.
It was half past four,
and there was nothing to do.
The newness of it all had long since worn off.


## Ballad of an Empty Table

It was very late at an empty table.
i had been watching the table do nothing.
for a moment
i thought i had something to say,
i thought about taking the pen out of my shirt
and drawing a snake on my arm
i thought about making two eyes on my fist
and calling them
                    EYES.
but dead men have better things to see with
and the Inspiration went under
like a fish floating on its back
in an illuminated bowl
suddenly gone dark.
i no longer knew what to say.
i tried to keep my eyes open,
watching the table do nothing.
the table was empty
and my hand was a cathedral upon it
and inside this cathedral
were the bones
of some famous saint
who had died
watching his table do nothing
and trying to remember the words.

but i knew there werent any words for this.
i tried to bring my hand down on the table
in anger,
in something
but my hand would not move.
the hand held me to the table.
i did not get angry.
the hand had me, that was all.
i tried to move a finger
to see if it was all right
to move a finger.
no
i couldnt do that.
i was starting to pray
although i wasnt saying anything
and i wasnt thinking anything
i was starting to pray
but i did not know it.
it was very late,
so this is how it is.
rifles and tables explode
pretty much the same.

# Patrick Lane

## Elephants

The cracked cedar
bunkhouse hangs behind me like a gray pueblo
in the sundown where I sit
to carve an elephant
from a hunk of brown soap
for the Indian boy
who lives in the village a mile back
in the bush.

The alcoholic truck-driver
and the cat-skinner sit beside
me with their eyes closed —
all of us waiting out the last hour
until we go back on the grade —

and I try to forget the forever
clank    clank    clank
across the grade
pounding stones and earth to powder
for hours in mosquito-darkness
of the endless cold mountain night.

The elephant takes form —
my knife caresses smooth soap
scaling off curls of brown
which the boy saves to take home
to his mother in the village.

Finished, I hand the carving to him
and he looks at the image of the great
beast for a long time
then sets it on dry cedar
and looks up at me:
                    What's an elephant?

he asks me
so I tell him of the elephants
and their jungles — the story
of the elephant graveyard
which no-one has ever found
and how the silent
animals of the rain-forest
go away to die somewhere
in the limberlost of distances
and he smiles at me

tells me of his father's
graveyard where his people have been
buried for years. So far back
no-one remembers when it started
and I ask him where the graveyard is
and he tells me it is gone
now where no-one will ever find it
buried under the grade of the new
highway.

## Sleep on the Fraser

Mountains have gathered in the distance
their skirts of fallen stone

I hang from the hooked tooth
of the Great Bear
and fall into the sky

## Treaty-Trip from Shulus Reservation

He leaned
against the dusty wall
with open pants
struggling with
drunken buttons
of his fly

his raven woman
knelt in the dirt
like some aged black
supplicant bird.
Hunched forward
she puked thin gruel
on his feet
and he raised his knee
struck her
in the face.

Beneath the dull lamp-yellow
outlined in counter-play
an Indian child
bounced her ball
against the flat red wall
her fluttering shadow
in wild macabre dance
a part of the tableau.

I hung there
in the sightless night
like a hooded
jesse-bound hawk
my quiet hammered breath
held in rhythmic beat
with the bouncing ball
that neatly caught
flew out
from the child's small hand
to thump
on the flat red wall.

## The Water-Truck

"You're fired, Lane"

he yelled and me lying
there and the truck
belching out great gouts
of water and me
half-drowned fifty feet
down from the edge
of the clay bank

and him running down
the ruts of my descent
grabbing me shaking
to my feet and throwing
me down in the mud again
blind without my glasses
where the truck spun out
its bald tires on the
slippery grade
                   nothing
like clay when its wet
you know
            and the boss
madder'n hell at me
for wrecking the truck
gasoline floating on
water and me lying
on wet stones and clay
looking for my glasses
blind as a bat
and the cat-skinner
beside the boss laughing
like hell and the boss
telling him to shutup

and the truck
I can still feel
rolling over and over
me inside holding on
to the spinning wheel
crashing down the bank
with five tons of water
behind bursting out
and the boss daring me
to get up and get out
his hands shaking and

     I find my glasses
finally locate him
standing there and
               "Fuck you"
I said
        "I quit"

## Love

*for Kathryn*

The book you made
for the teacher
is beautiful
              full
of drawings you have
made of your queen

The colour of her
skin is yellow
her nakedness
like a moon
low on the horizon

Is it something
she asked for?

No
It's a gift I made her

## Mountain Oysters

Kneeling in the sheepshit
he picked up the biggest of the new rams,
brushed the tail aside,
slit the bag,
tucked the knackers in his mouth
and clipped the cords off clean —

the ram stiff
with a single wild scream

as the tar went on
and he spit the balls in a bowl.

That's how we used to do it
when I was a boy.
It's no more gawdam painful
than any other way
and you can't have rams fightin,
slammin it up every nanny . . .

and enjoyed them with him,
cutting delicately
into the deep-fried testicles.

Mountain oysters make you strong

he said
while out in the field
the rams stood holding their pain,
legs fluttering like blue hands
of old tired men.

## Loving She Stood Apart

loving she stood apart
and looked at me wanting
her and afraid she was
of the wanting to need
me watching her from
where I lay on the bed
as she undressed

and turned her back
to me    undressed her
back was smooth    the
angle of her hip so
I could touch her
holding my hand beside me
feet from where she was
her hands soft fingers
reaching out to me
from where they rested
on her shoulders afraid
to turn around and see me
see her eyes

"Turn out the light"

she said and when I
made no move to move
my eyes to blackness
and the loss she said

"please . . ."

so quietly my mind
shut out the sight
and I was blind to
her but O the night

## Surcease

Here in this car is surcease from a thousand dead —
a woman and a bottle and the rain.

Used car chrome crumbles into dust
and broken windows stain with smears of rust;
each rock-scarred shivered pane
creased with a crust of red. Your eyes
in darkness will never see why you're afraid
and why I'm drunk.

Only hours can drain away the sudden
years, pits I've placed my dead in.
I don't want words from you.

Tonight I want to turn with you to neon,
blue as the stiff veins under your tongue —
and don't say: Give it time
say nothing,
to hell with time.
Take off your clothes. Hang
your breasts in my eyes. I want
to ride on your body through this rain
and celebrate the darkness and my pain . . .
forget the past.

Play with me gently, woman, I'm made of glass.
I could break so easily.


## Gray Silk Twisting

I stick my tongue in you,
move like a great fluid worm
eating out your soul. At night
I was told our souls leave our bodies
through our mouths
but I know it leaves every hole
like gray silk twisting,
tasting of earth.

I enter you this way,
my eyes in your hair,
my fingers gripping the smooth
lips of you. Without speaking
you wrap your gray inside me
as I dance
finally thigh to thigh
attached to you by hooks,
tearing me as I come.


## Beware the Months of Fire
## They Are Twelve and Contain a Year

Hung from a stone branch of city wall
a red cloth bleeds ragged in the rain.
A pallid fire in the winter seacoast night.
I see the skirt of a woman walking proud,
hesitant in the crumpled shade of light,
moving to some destination I'll never know.
The casual cruelty of a street-lamp
breaks down the rain.

A red cloth drifts triumphant
over ramparts of garbage
where boys wield swords and symbols
in the wet storms of war.
But there was a woman walking proud,
revealing a touch of leg where her dress was
and there are children sleeping
behind these walls of rain.

Beware the months of fire.
They are twelve and contain a year
of children sleeping and a walking woman
and a torn dress like a lost tongue.
Now just to leave it there in the night,
threaded to mould. A thing for birds to plunder
and mice to find wrapped around their bones.

# Irving Layton

## Aran Islands

*Dun Aengus*

High walls ... of stones;
man-humbling cliff and shattering sea;
ramparts:
trenches of stone, fierce four of them
and in-between
prehistory's barbed wire, *cheveux de frise*
... of stones.

Enclosing a mist.

Gone are the defenders;
gone, they who attacked.

Nothing here:
only mist
and blue-grey stones.

*Cliffs of Moher*

At last, as in a dream,
I've come to the cliffs
from where God hurls down
His enemies, every one.

Rat-faced cunning mercer's
with a rat's delight:
all, all who are dead of soul,
male and female.

See, their polls open like flowers
on the black rocks below;
their brains dance with the foam
on a green wave's tow.

*Kilmurvey*

Low are the hills, a mere rise
in the ground, grey with stones and green;
Stand anywhere and you can trace
outlines with your new-found eyes
of stone fences delicate as lace:
Stand anywhere and you can be seen.

## The Haunting

Why without cease do I think of a bold youth
        national origin unimportant or racial Peruvian
Russian Irish Javanese he has fine clear eyes
honest smiling mouth a pat for a child's head
talks to old women and helps them cross the street
        is friendly with mainliners anarchs and nuns
Cote St. Luc housewives their ruined husbands and brats
optometrists sign painters lumpenproletarians dumping
their humps into coffee cups plotting revenge
and clerics who've made out of Christ a bearded faggot

From the rotating movement of a girl's beautiful
        buttocks he draws energy as from the sun
(O lovely revolving suns on St. Catherine street)
and from breasts and perfumed shoulders and hair
Piccadilly Wilhelmstrasse Fifth Avenue Rue St. Germain
        the suns go rolling on luminous hoops pinwheels
handsprings and somersaults of desirable flesh
the bold youth with wide-apart happy eyes
stepping lightly over blossoming asphalt graves is running
after them touching a child's head smiling to old women

Why don't I ever meet him face to face?
sometimes I've seen him stepping off a bus
but when I've caught up with him he's changed
into a bourgeois giving the two-fingered peace sign
or a poet shouting love as if it were a bomb
on damp days into an office clerk smelling of papers
is he somebody's doppelganger? an emanation or
shadow I see taking shape near a plateglass window?
who is he? he haunts me like an embodied absence
and as if I had lived all my life in arrears


**For Anna**

You wanted the perfect setting
for your old world beauty, postwar Hungarian:
a downtown Toronto bar sleazy
with young whores pimps smalltime racketeers

remembering boyhood Xmases in Elmira
plus one poet pissed to the gills
by turns raving or roaring like an acidhead
then suddenly silent like the inside of a glass

I'm sure you placed him there as camera
as incorruptible juror or witness
but who can give report of a miracle?
having seen it what struck dumb can he tell?

and to whom? they who pressed around you
were converted and left off dreaming of murder
or rape in public parks/some cried for happiness . . .
they outside or riding the subways will never believe

Now I know everything which happened
that night was your creation/you invented
it all by cupping your elegant proper hands
then letting the night escape like a black moth

that shattered the fantastic radiance of your head
into a thousand glints and scintillations
transfiguring bottles whisky glasses even the leers
on aroused Canadian clerks fingering their wallets

and making me run after you to discover
whether you are a woman with blood and orifices
one may after all love and if the answer is yes
whether you will warm my aging limbs as a lover


## Ohms

ohms
is such a beautiful word

soft as marshmallow in the mouth
as a lover's sigh

hearing it for the first time
in Physics 6
I was electrified

it was like my first kiss
my first piece of ass
but cleaner purer

since then I've loved ohms
passionately
especially ohms of resistance

if you try to say the word
in anger
or vindictively
you can't ohms is pure poetry

bellow it
it comes out a muted cry of pain:
the sound the universe makes

yet poets have written
about owls yes about owls many times

nightingales snakes daffodils bridges
graveyards
but not about ohms

therefore I've written this poem
and now wish to add only this:

ohms is immortal
chaste and lovely as a rainbow
it will delight our seed
on Venus Jupiter Mars

when the great Florentine
even he
is gibberish to their ears


**For Natalya Correia**

You possess the sturdy elegance of a cannon
and move always with the authority
of someone about to capture a city

Are indisputably beyond the vanity
of attention and compliments
like famous statues fixed in permanent triumph

Who in aloof approving silence
or unending melancholy disdain
regard their admirers at the crowded base

If you dispense anger or annoyance
it is as if doing so you establish
the existence of those who provoked them

And entertain each day those certainties
acclamation and gratified desire foster
in a voluptuous and talented woman

I admire wholeheartedly the egotism
with which you half stretch out on your couch
like a glistening female sealion

And pour without my permission
wine from my wineglass into your own
fanning with delighted self-absorption

The smoke curling about your impressive head
or jab ebony cigaret holder into space
as if to poke chrysolites from their hiding place


## Osip Mandelshtam

*(1891–1940)*

I once did an hour-long TV show reading
from your *Stamen* and *Trivia:* out there
were my compatriots who had never before
heard of your name and pain, your nightmare fate;
of course the impresario spoke impressively
about your stay in Paris where you mastered
the French symbolists, your skill as translator
(what pre-Belsen Jew hadn't promiscuously
shacked up with five or six gentile cultures)
the Hellenic feeling in your prose and poems
— to be brief, he filled in the familiar picture
of enlightened Jew ass bared to the winds

But when that self-taught master symbolist
il miglior fabbro put you on his list of touchables
that was the end; you perished in the land waste
of Siberia, precisely where no one knows and few care
for in that stinking imperium whose literature
you adorned like a surrealist Star of David

you're still an unclaimed name, a Jewish ghost
who wanders occasionally into enclaves
of forlorn intellectuals listening
for the ironic scrape of your voice
in the subversive hum of underground presses

I know my fellow-Canadians, Osip;
they forgot your name and fate as swiftly
as they learned them, switching off
the contorted image of pain with their sets,
choosing a glass darkness to one which starting
in the mind covers the earth in permanent eclipse;
so they chew branflakes and crabmeat gossip make love
take out insurance against fires and death
while our poetesses explore their depressions
in delicate complaints regular as menstruation
or eviscerate a dead god for metaphors;
the men-poets displaying codpieces of wampum,
the safer legends of prairie Indian and Eskimo

Under a sour and birdless heaven
TV crosses stretch across a flat Calvary
and plaza storewindows give me
the blank expressionless stare of imbeciles:
this is Toronto, not St. Petersburg on the Neva;
though seas death and silent decades separate us
we yet speak to each other, brother to brother;
your forgotten martyrdom has taught me scorn
for hassidic world-savers without guns and tanks:
they are mankind's gold and ivory toilet bowls
where brute or dictator relieves himself
when reading their grave messages to posterity
— let us be the rapturous eye of the hurricane
flashing the Jew's will, his mocking contempt for slaves

# Don L. Lee

**Nigerian Unity / or little niggers killing little niggers**

*for brothers Christopher Okigbo & Wole Soyinka*

suppose those
who made
wars
had to fight them?

it's called blackgold.
& you,
my brothers / former warriors
who use to own the nights
that
knew no boarders
have acquired strings on yr / minds
& have knowingly sold yr / our / mothers.
there are no more tears.
tears will not stop bullets.
the dead don't cry,
the dead just grow; good crop this year,
wouldn't u say.

it's called blackgold
& u fight blindly,
swinging at yr / own mid-nights,
at yr / own children of tomorrow.

come    one    come    two
against the middle is
a double feature starring the man from u.n.c.l.e.
with a nigger on his back
who played ping-pong with christ
and won.

little niggers
killing
little niggers: ontime / intime / outoftime
        theirtime / otherpeople'stime as
        niggers killed niggers everytime.

suppose those
who made
wars
had to fight them?

blackgold is not
the newnigger:
with a british accent
called me "old chap" one day,
i rubbed his skin
it didn't come off. even him surprised.

him
another pipe-smoking faggot
who lost his balls in
a double-breasted suit
walking thru a nadinola commercial
with a degree in european history.
little nigger
choked himself with a hippy's tie
his momma didn't even know him /
        she thought he was a TWA flashback or
        something out of a polka-dot machine.
he
cursed at her in perfect english
called her:
Mother-Dear.

WANTED      WANTED
    black warriors to go south
    to fight in Africa's mississippi.

go south young man.

everybody missed that train,
except one sister.
she wanted to fight the realenemy
but
she was "uneducated,"
wore the long-dress
talked the native tongue
& had a monopoly on blackbeauty.
when we met — she smiled & said: "i'm the true gold,
         i'm the real-gold."

suppose those
who made
wars
had to fight them?

the real blackgold
was there before the drill,
before the dirty-eyed,
before the fence-builders,
before the wells,
before the british accent,
before christ,
before air condition,
before the cannon,
the real blackgold: was momma & sister; **is** momma &
  sister.
was there before the "educated,"
before the pig-eaters,
before the cross-wearers,
before the pope,
before the nigger-warriors.
the real blackgold
was the first warrior.

go south young man.

little niggers
killing
little niggers.
the weak against the weak.
the ugly against the ugly.
the powerless against the powerless.
the realpeople becoming unpeople
& brothers we have more in common
than pigmentation & stupidity.
that same old two-for-one
was played on 47th & ellis —
invented on 125 & lenox
and now is double-dealing from
the mangrove swamps to the savannah grassland;
2 niggers for the price of nothing.

newnigger
lost his way
a whi-te girl gave him direction
him still lost
she sd whi-te / he thought bite
been eating everything in sight
including himself.

suppose those
who made
wars
had to fight them?

the lone ranger got a new tonto
he's "brown" with a Ph.D. in
psy-chol-o-gy
& still walks around with
holes
in his brain.
losthismind.

saw him the other day
with his head across some railroad tracks —
tryin to get an untan.
will the real jesus christ
**please** stand up
and take a bow;
u got niggers tryin to be trains.

trained well.
european-african took a
**double**
at oxford.
wears ban-lon underwear & whi-te socks,
has finally got the killer's eye,
join the deathbringers club
& don't want more than two children.

the real blackgold
will be crippled,
raped,
and killed
in
that
order.

i will miss
the joy
of calling her
sister

go south young man.

suppose those
who made
wars
had to fight **you.**

## Black Sketches

*1*

i
was five
when
mom & dad got married
& i
didn't realize that
i
was illegitimate
until i started
school.

*2*

i was at
the airport
& had
to use the
men's room
real bad
& didn't have a
dime.

*3*

somebody
made a
mistake (they said)
&
sent the
peace corps to
europe.

4

went to cash
my
1968 tax refund
&
the check bounced;
insufficient funds.

5

i
read the
newspapers today
&
thought that
everything
was
all right.

6

nat turner
returned
&
killed
william styron
&
his momma too.

7

ed brooke
sat at his
desk
crying & slashing
his wrist
because somebody
called him
black.

*8*

general westmoreland
was transferred
to the
westside of chicago
&
he lost
there too.

*9*

in 1959
my mom
was dead at the
age of
35
& nobody thought it unusual;
not even
me.

*10*

in 1963
i
became black
& everyone thought it unusual;
even me.

*11*

the american dream:
       nigger bible in
       every hotel;
       iceberg slim (pimp) getting
       next to julia;
       & roy wilkins on
       the mod squad.

**Assassination**

it was wild.
the
bullet hit high.
        (the throat-neck)
& from everywhere:
        the motel, from under bushes and cars,
        from around corners and across streets,
        out of the garbage cans and from rat holes
        in the earth
they came running.
with
guns
drawn
they came running
toward the King —
        all of them
        fast and sure —
as if
the King
was going to fire back.
they came running,
fast and sure,
in the
wrong
direction.


**Man and Woman**

*for Earnie, 1964*

two baths in one day!
at first i thought that you
just wanted to be clean.
then, u pulled the lights off
& the darkness took me away from my book.
lightly,
i asked about your perfume
u answered,

& added that u splashed it in unknown & strange places
and again lightly,
i asked,
if the perfume was *black.*
at first
our backs touched & we both played sleep.
u turned toward me
& the warmth of yr / blood rushes over me    as
u throw yr / left leg over my left leg
& get dangerous, very dangerous with yr / left hand.
the soul-station comes on automatically
with the aid of yr / right hand.
ike & tina turner are singing "get back"
from yr / touch i flinch and say,
listen to the record, woman!
you don't and i don't    while
"get back" is in rhythm
with the shaking of the bed
that's
mixed with our soft voices
that undoubtedly are heard unconfused through
thin walls.


## We Walk the Way of the New World

*1*

we run the dangercourse.
the way of the stocking caps & murray's grease.
(if u is modern u used duke greaseless hair pomade)
jo jo was modern / an international nigger
                born: jan. 1, 1863 in new york, mississippi.
his momma was mo militant than he was / is
jo jo bes no instant negro
his development took all of 106 years
& he was the first to be stamped "made in USA"
where he arrived bow-legged a curve ahead of the 20th
        century's new weapon: television.
which invented, "how to win and influence people"
& gave jo jo his how / ever look: however u want me.

we discovered that with the right brand of cigarettes
that one, with his best girl,
cd skip thru grassy fields in living color
& in slow-motion: Caution: niggers, cigarette smoking
                will kill u & yr / health.
& that the breakfast of champions is: blackeyed peas & rice.
& that God is dead & Jesus is black and last seen on 63rd
            street in a gold & black dashiki, sitting in a pink
            hog speaking swahili with a pig-latin accent.
& that integration and coalition are synonymous,
& that the only thing that really mattered was:
        who could get the highest on the least or how to expand
        & break one's mind.

in the coming world
new prizes are
to be given
we *ran* the dangercourse.
now, it's a silent walk / a careful eye
jo jo is there
to his mother he is unknown
(she accepted with a newlook: what wd u do if someone
        loved u?)
jo jo is back
& he will catch all the new jo jo's as they wander in & out
and with a fan-like whisper say: you ain't no
                tourist
                and Harlem ain't for
                sight-seeing, brother.

2

Start with the itch and there will be no scratch. Study
        yourself.
Watch yr / every movement as u skip thru-out the
        southside of
        chicago.
be hip to yr / actions

our dreams are realities
traveling the nature-way.
we meet them
at the apex of their utmost
meanings / means;
we walk in cleanliness
down state st / or Fifth Ave.
& wicked apartment buildings shake
as their windows announce our presence
as we jump into the interior
& cut the day's evil away.

We walk in cleanliness
the newness of it all
becomes us
our women listen to us
and learn.
We teach our children thru
our actions.

We'll become owners of the   New World
the New World.
will run it as unowners
for
we will live in it too
& will want to be remembered
as   realpeople.

# Lyn Lifshin

**Beryl**

My father in his
sister's dark house
chanting like a
Jew. Candles,
Friday wine

Everything there had a
peculiar heavy
richness
flushed cheeks and
velvet, amber shawls.
A fat smell of praying

In Vermont in
rooms plain grey and
wooden
I remember him sitting
those nights without
a word and
how he stood in the park,
listened to chestnuts dropping.
But not much else

only just now
I'm saying
Beryl, his
sleek Hebrew name,
I didn't even know
I knew it

Is that what he
wanted back

or what?


## You Understand the Requirements

We are
sorry to have to
regret to
tell you
sorry sorry
regret sorry that you have
failed

your hair should have been
piled up higher

you have failed to
pass failed
your sorry
regret your
final hair comprehensive
exam satisfactorily
you understand the requirements

you understand we are
sorry final

and didn't look as professional
as desirable
or sorry dignified
and have little enough
sympathy for 16th century
sorry english anglicanism

we don't know doctoral
competency what to think and
regret you will sorry not
be able to stay
or finish

final regret your disappointment
the unsuccessfully completed best
wishes for the future
it has been a
regret sorry the requirements
the university policy
    please don't call us.


## The Way Sun Keeps Falling Away from Every Window

This is the kind
of marriage they live in:
split and stuffed with
terrible dead furniture,
he doing anything he
can to make her
happy, saving up a
big stiff
bankroll while she drowns
in hills of carpet
wanting what she doesn't
know he's going to buy
automatic brooms
for poking
deep in all her
corners, machines to make her
panties whirl at varied
speeds and circles, bouncing
but it all stays
wrong it isn't what
either of them wanted. Take me she wants
to scream, even on the
staircase, even in the daylight
nuzzle down my stomach
with all your tongues    but
instead she talks of oranges and lettuce
and mornings orders
rape from the milkman, boxes
thick with cream and fears each night that time of
grey teeth, that her nipples

suddenly fall like wrinkled lemons, dreams
a parade of hair and cocks, hot scrotum marching
grinding against her
in through her flannel crotch,
wild in her
vagina — balls like wet suns muscling her
flesh, great mounds of dampness, the
dream exploding birds
in all her mouths    her teeth are clogged with
sperm and feathers
and she wakes, longing, startled,
her lips pressed thin,
wondering of stains they could leave,
              a smell of something
that is animal.
But the sheets are dryer than leaves
nothing has been
touched, the hair between their thighs stays smooth,
unruffled.
Sun falls away from every window
and a noise keeps biting under the meat of her eyes,
her throat wants something more than
glass and linen.
In closets of shoes and old guitars she
waits, is touching where he never
enters, falls lost among the lonely shoes and
              rusty dresses,
waiting, but almost certain that they can
              never really come to be together.


**Waiting, the Hallways under Her Skin**
**Thick with Dreamchildren**

Lace grows in her eyes like
fat weddings,
she is pretty, has been baking

bisquits of linen to stuff into his mouth
all her life,

waiting for him. The hallways
under skin are thick with dreamchildren.

Who he is hardly matters, her rooms
stay for him,

her body crying to be taken
with rings and furniture, tight behind doors

in a wave of green breath and wild rhythm,
in a bed of
lost birds and feathers,

smiling, dying.


## On the New Road

red sumac presses
against the windshield,
tires moan

Your wife dreams
you are guilty,

I button and unbutton
what I feel


## Family 8

Another uncle
was a pathological liar
but so gentle with whores,

bringing them dogs and flowers.
Law school then a cluttered
five to dime, mainly toys and
needles but under the counter

squirting from split knees,
maiden juice it said,
just press the button.

Twelve years of Sundays
were always with the Irish girl
but secretly, that her iceblue eyes
the family shouldn't see, and

slow afternoons in the rented room
till at fifty love grew thin
so he married the rabbi's daughter,
but he never had a son.


## Not Quite Spring

Baby you know I get high
on you, come back with me
whispering in her ear
it was all she could do to say
no, spring leaves budding,
his hand on her breast
crocus smell and
everything unfolding
she gasping I want, I
would but instead hurrying
back to the windowless room
where she locks the heavy door.
Lemons are rotting on her pillow,
she studies her nipples,
nyloned crotch in mirror
then hugs her huge body to sleep.

## For a Friend

Leaving beer and apples
on the window
for later
lying together those nights
till four,
talking
everybody must have thought
that we were
lovers
your red mustache in the blanket
smell of your cigarette in my hair
white thighs in the mountains
getting bombed on the sky

But when I stand
back I don't recognize
myself or
you love
who got into my skirt
and blood
before I knew
your name and then
wanted to be
mostly friends

Those 3 weeks
everything that moved in my
bones stretched
toward you,
I wanted to take you inside me that deep
your crooked smile, Russian
eyes but you
grew into the desk, your
back a wall

What were
you feeling those
nights we undressed, then
in the dark
you asked who else I could
talk to like this
while I was wondering what to do
with feelings I
couldn't use,
your face
so close to mine
it chilled me

**To Poem**

all night
you banged
in my head
poking your fingers
thru me, hot for
blood and then
in the morning
stretching out on
the table
flaunting your muscles
when you knew there wasn't time.
Later in the car
you made me dizzy.
but worse, how you
made my love jealous
perching in my hair
with those stiff wings.
and now, bastard
alone with me finally
the chance to
scares you off

155     *Lyn Lifshin*

## Pulling Out

First their eyes
pull toward new underwater
places, a terrible dark
gill catching her attention,

she didn't know he was like this,
heart scooped, full of glassware and
tin. But she still wants him
breathing in her

body, grows new lips and muscles, gold
mirrors in her side until he
moans that he can't stand
her spying. And their mouths fill with

stones. But they go on
anyway in this water that keeps
everything slow, his metal
penis still moving in her, the holes

in her side leak so slowly
it's hard to tell what's
lost. Only, they're
having this trouble, the floor slides

away, they can't tell where they
stand, her thighs won't
hold him. Words
come heavy too and hang

like blood sealed in plastic. Love
is certainly pealing away
and all she wanted
was something warm, green

water to flow inside her body,
smoke her heart.
But he slips from the places she dreamed
he would know, her gills are so

lonely — yes it's just like
any movie    run it
backwards    see the lips pull out, bodies
twisting upright.

Arms float without any direction.
Salt comes and it's
all shell and separation,
love jerking down their throats, hooks

and weeds taking them, spreading in
their hair. All their reflections
breaking. Torn pieces of
her glass scrape his metal    she

misses his bones but
they're both bloated from being in this
water too long
                o let's get out of

here she cries    couldn't
we live in a
mountain    in a glacier    on a green
stone somewhere

but something in them has been turning
so hard    clots of coral
loss so brittle
that they break, and splinter

so raggedly
nobody can touch them

# Dick Lourie

## The Gift

"here we are at the river"    I said to no one
wondering about "the gift of metaphor" as Elaine calls it
Homer had it    and surely others since then
while I sit on a rock    feet in the moving water
is it missing from my poems?    they seem so plain

I can only say "I am at the river
                    water moving    fish
                    my wife sleeping in the afternoon"

to say it like that is such a — Bob's brother-in-law
thought my poems sounded like newspaper
articles    maybe that's true    but somewhere
I have as much metaphor as I need:
                    "sitting on a rock midstream    I love my wife
                    sun on the water    in / out of clouds
                    next year we'll begin having babies
                    my feet in the moving water
                    the darkness of the water against the far bank
                    the brightness of the water flat under the sun
                    the clarity of the water over the small stones
                    the movement of the water forever"

there it is:    I give you my gift.

## Thinking of You

about one month before my thirty-third
birthday I finally decided I
have to write poems more often than every
six weeks    that goes for you too    you know you'll have
to decide sometime    do it now    it may
be too late at the edge of thirty-three
for me it's almost winter before I make up
my mind    the sun setting at half-past four
by now    and to go out even in the
day I need a coat    please listen    do it
even if it's only rain as you cross the
mountain    or being scared by the sight of
the president's face at a news conference
or quarrels with your lover    do it    poems
more often    even if it's only that you
come around a turn on to the plain and see
New Paltz in the distance like phony Camelot
and the pumpkins dead in the roadside fields


## September 30

last night we slept in Miami in the house of
my grandfather    end of our journey from Taos
adobe    a village six hundred years    my grand-
mother heating coffee for us    my grandfather
taking a look at our indian drum    then we
went to bed in their house    and I recognized things
a Persian Carpet    a lamp    a painting    which had
surrounded me when as a child I lived with them
parts of themselves they took along    Brooklyn
to New Jersey to old age in Florida    so
we went to sleep    the tropical night    insects like
birds and in the morning I was in love all over
with my wife    my new wife    what skin what hair
     what eyes

## Telegram

leather belt     white shirt     black pants
army shoes     the night     woman
my life     my death     never
stars beyond mist     or     through mist

## Stumbling

nights and days we stumble over each other
even living in the country doesn't help
we've learned the keeping apart which is half of
living together    but to be in the same
place at the same time    touch    eat    make love    somehow
this eludes us    instead we eat food without
tasting    on our walks one of us is always ten
feet ahead and behind    making love I am
clumsy you say    you are dull I reply    and
any touching isn't caress or even
coming to blows    but like each one trying to
dance alone in the same place at the same time

## The Dream about Junior High School in America

the busses are bright yellow    and have brought
seventh and eighth graders to the flat new
brick school on the suburban outskirts of
town:    now about a hundred of the boys
and girls have gathered to hear a talk by
a young man blinded a few years ago
in an accident:    fascinated they
ask about the dog at his side    and he
describes their training together    it is
noticeable he does not wear dark glasses
the blind eyes as if naked and he turns
his face toward questioners as if he is
looking at them    "are you interested
in sports?"    "Oh yes    I used to hunt a lot"
he says    turning that face again in that
strange way    "and now I collect guns    Smith and
Wesson pistols    and Winchester rifles".

## Getting a Poem in the Rain

I eat my cereal with a sliced peach
this is early September in the Rondout
Valley:    fog and rain in the cool morning
I drive over the mountain and down the
other side    through Gardiner    where there is
mist on a roadside pond and a small fine rain
through Ardonia into Clintondale.
there in the town hall is an old German
man sitting at a desk in silence    his
eyes are blue    and puffed    and clear    he takes my name
and tells me at great length about apples


## Pearl Harbor Day 1970

just this morning I signed the contract
to become a 7th grade English
teacher    included are liberal
New York State retirement benefits

and the choice of monthly payments or
a lump sum for my wife in case of
my death while on the job
                    it was        last
night we visited with two old friends
soldiers of the revolution    we
all had dinner and tried to find some
appropriate music to dance to
fifties rock & roll was not the thing

at length we settled on my tape of
the Stones    and shook the floor of the old
house for almost an hour

                              our friends have
decided to leave the city for
physical health reasons and settle
on the cape    we talked about
being in ten years middle-aged and perhaps

that by then we could live communal
in Vermont    each couple or person
their own house    yet organized around
a common space    big kitchen for meals
together    books    music    life with friends

and today signing for my new job
I realized that by then if still
alive I might be able to get
some of the liberal retirement
benefits the state provides    it would

ease things somewhat    we would all be to-
gether perhaps in Vermont living
but it didn't make me feel better


## Sharks

I dreamed of a shark following us    two
sharks following us as we walk through waist-
deep water    my wife and I    they're playful
as porpoises    nuzzling like dogs    I am
afraid if we should bleed they will smell it
and kill us    deliberately staying
calm    because she doesn't realize they're
sharks    I open the door of our car and
suggest we get in    as usual the
floor of the car is filthy with coffee
containers    newspapers    screwdriver    flash-
light    broken thermos bottles    we sit in
the car    somehow the sharks get up on the
roof    they look at us through    reach for us through
the open windows

# David McFadden

**Kicking from Centre Field**

The butcher, a bald guy
who grew his side-hair long & combed it up
over the top of his head daringly
was slicing my bologna (39¢ lb.)
& in my imagination I was running
his slightly off-axis head
through the slicing machine
realizing it wouldn't be any good for food
wouldn't look good & would taste worse.

& the next butcher was helping
an elderly amused woman select her steaks
& she was so fussy & agonizingly slow
that my butcher's eyes & mine
briefly touched with a charity
for all flesh-eaters
          & a clarity
that pierced through to the other world.

**Art's Variety**

*A poem should touch the hearer with a sense of his own
weakness & should institute some comparison between
mankind & flowers.*
                    *E. M. Forster*

      She was so small & pretty
      my heart broke & breaking
      tried to determine her age.
      I wondered if she wore a bra
      then dimly pickt out the straps.

I bought toothpaste, fuses
& a twin-pack of lightbulbs
& she said "Are you sure
there's two bulbs in there?"
Then opened the pack to check.
"I'd hate to have you go home . . .

& find yourself with one bulb."
She's somewhere between 12 & 30
I thought, amazed at the delicate
fences around her, the tiny bones
full of marrow, the fleshy moat

& her age so indeterminable
like a tiny tree suspended upside down
deep in the centre of her brain.

## The External Element

When I was a kid
I had kites & they always
ended entangled in trees

but stronger than the kite memories
is a dream I had at the time
in which my mother climbed a tree
to retrieve one of my smashed kites
& me crying: Ma, don't bother!

& up there she lost balance
fell, landing across the high tension wires
& was electrocuted, the black cinder
of my Ma falling softly to the ground.

For weeks after I couldn't do enough
to help my mother,
    I was an ideal son
for over a month

     & even now
I hate poetry with a passion
& write poems.

## We Love You the Way You Are

*Madame, you don't realize the
look on my face
is not the way I feel inside*
      *Mike Bloomfield*

1

The ignorant dawn of William Butler Yeats
& all the things I do for you
& all the photos & portraits Yeats left;
it's like wondering what sex is the sun
wondering what Mr Yeats was like
in physical presence, & his poems?
He couldn't have been that bad.

He was probably like his ignorant dawn,
grey & threatening to bedazzle any time
but never quite doing it,
cold & passionate yet his poems
are so warm & dull
yet I keep falling through the wordtraps
& into a realization of myself
in another time & place,
Ireland in the first third of this century
the world at a time when probably
only one person (also Irish) (Joyce)
knew what was going on.

What was going on?
Rabbits were being shot,
cities torn down & reerected, Finnegans Wake
& Yeats was taking a step back from Paradise
voluntarily, & pretending it was lost forever
& violently hammering a poem into shape
the opposite of what he was really like
cold & passionate, & his poems so warm & dull.

165    *David McFadden*

**2**

My daughter Jennifer at 15 months
is so warm & affectionate it scares me.
I'm sitting on the floor listening to music
& she's suddenly behind me, arms around my neck
beating time on my chest, laughing.
I turn around & her eyes light,
she starts climbing me
in a brilliant blue shimmering illumination.

I remember 15 months ago
Joan in the Labor Room & me
standing there like a tree rooted helplessly
& she's wheeled into the Delivery Room
& I'm wheeled down to the Father's Room
where I can observe the delivery room door

Then Dr. W. C. Williams, long string bean
with a head like a baseball, comes out
strides down the hall toward me,
closer & closer & now he's almost here
& now he's shaking my hand
& I'm pumping his arm like a pump
bring the cool news up from eternity
& here I think it's coming now
& here it is: Congratulations!
I pump harder. You've got a lovely
daughter! My head pops open like a pod.
I pump harder, hoping to find her
heavenly name. I keep pumping.
It was an extremely easy birth
says the doctor, & the baby's eyes
were wide open, staring at me
as she was born, very strange,
I've never seen that before.

Where the rabbit rested
is only the outline of its form
in the grass, said Yeats
who now is dead.

His form is gone forever
I won't believe a portrait
I won't believe his poems.

But I'll half believe that he
was a previous incarnation of me
& a thousand other fish in the sea.
& standing still rooted like a tree
sorting out the billions of tiny dots
the good grey news streams up from eternity

William Butler Yeats is you & me for Jesus' sake
& Jennifer is the daughter of Willie Blake.


## The Day of the Pancreas

*Feb 19 / 69*

This morn my friend Al mentioned his wife had taken a job
& the babysitter they'd hired was a diabetic.
This afternoon I attended the Peel County Courthouse
& Crown Attorney Gerhardt mentioned he
was a diabetic,
              & one of the defense witnesses,
Mrs. Woolcock, mentioned she was a diabetic.
This evening my mother said she'd met that old-time
    disc jockey
Joe Van Popple & he'd mentioned his diabetes
was being complicated with glaucoma.

& in today's paper there's an article
about new canvassing techniques being used
by the Canadian Diabetes Association
& a letter in Dr. Alvarez's Medical Column
from S.T.F., 68, is woefully worried
about his diabetes-glaucoma problem.


## It's a Different Story When You're Going Into the Wind

The kids are asleep
The dog is in the cellar
Joan is at her sister's

I got that much written & the phone rang
It was Joan telling me she met her sister's
        new boy friend George.

The dog & me went for a walk earlier
In the park we ran & shouted & barked
We took the long way home, the crescent moon
shining through purple clouds above the tennis court.

The dog is like a politician always hedging.
We stopped on the sidewalk & looked in the window
of this one house. At first I thought the three people
were all watching TV, then I saw it wasn't a TV
but the guest of honor, a real human being
sitting on a chair in the corner, three pairs of eyes
on him.


## The Fiddlehead

*for Kitty*

O my life is so simple & the world
so unutterably complicated, like a kid
thinking about how the universe began.

Thinking about myself as well as I can
with the cat purring like a pneumatic drill
crawling around my head & shoulders

I'd say my head is empty as an old beer bottle
found in the woods, you pick it up curious
& get a faint whiff of last year's beer

& a strong sense of woodsy secrets,
the spiritual processes of trees, popping seedpods
the daily sun, rotting layers of loam

bottle like a discarded espionage device
anchored glumly in the swirling great joy.


**Upon Looking at a Book of Astrology**

The twelve elements in slow orbit
around the outer limits of my brain
& I touch what I can of each
according to my touch like anyone
any one position on my body

Eternity has 12 stops along my body,
who could ask for anything more?

Twelve eyes moving slowly along
& into my body

Slowly tapping the minds of the gods:
Dale Walker of New Orleans Louisiana
sends in today's question: Of what
possible use are the stars?

The stars are storehouses of intelligence,
testicles of psycho-electric human unfoldment

The stars actually do exist, just as they are
in the heavens, placed by he-who-now-ignores (?)

Roy Kiyooka using his *Guide to the Heavens*
to assign titles to his paintings, paintings
that look at me with the eyes
of cats or babies
                    or astronomical symbols unblinking

I started to cast my own astrological chart
but the information in the book was incomplete
just enough to see that with a bit more information
I could go on & on forever

like the writing of poems
going on & on from day to day
with an explosive touch of communication
some time in the 24th century

a molecule of new meaning
my contribution to the stars
fathering a race of fish-tailed goats
raising a new pacific continent

& anyway today in modern 20th century
the stars are so dim, skies so distant
hurts my eyes to look that high
Gazing at the heavens is the purpose of life
& it's so hard to be purposeful

but even someone like me, hopeless
neither a sailor nor an architect
can see human nature in the stars
a strange nocturnal glowing in my fellows
                    unverbalized power
unseen, unsuspected, complicated, unspeakable
loops, billion-hookt principles undreamed-of.

## Pop

I open the door & walk in
& little Alison comes running toward me
she has a limp yellow balloon in her hand
& asks me to inflate it, daddy

It's almost bed time & she
is wearing her pink nightgown
candystriped white & pink

& the balloon has printed on itself
in neat little type
FIGHT CYSTIC FIBROSIS
GIVE A CHILD THE BREATH OF LIFE

I blow the balloon up & the type
increases in size about 10 times
(goes quickly from little to large)
(grows like magic)

(it would be nice if books
came in adjustable type
& nice if I could blow myself
up into John Keats' size

I've been reading John Keats

one day John coughed on to his sleeve
a little blood, he was 24
& knew death was nigh
(149 years ago this month)
so he wrote a letter to each of his friends
saying I'm going to die now

I tell Alison to keep the balloon
away from the cat & and she says why?
& I say 'cause the cat'll break it
& you will cry

A little later I hear from the kitchen
that characteristic POP of a burst balloon
followed by no crying.

# Larry Mollin

**Tubes**

*for Annie*

The subway messes me up
                    sexually
Shooting thru the tubes I
                    get excited
But just when I really get a good thing going
Like from 59th to 125th on the "A"
I get hung up on transfers and locals
Expresses rape my intentions
And those impotent gum machines
Masturbate my mind.

Oh
Maybe someday
        I'll not be tempted by those slut machines
        And I'll buy tokens in advance and
        Know the mystery of the "A"

But until then
I think I make love better in the country
Where my mind's not hustling
And my body knows nothing
But the inner passage of your soft transit
                                    no transfers
And me
        my own conductor.

## Signature

when we slept
we slept on
torn sheets
and we were rough
and they tore more
and we loved it

but now
only i sleep on
what's left of
these torn sheets
and in the mornings
i find blood rings
stamped
from mattress buttons
all over
my body


## Wash Day

doing my wash
isn't all bad
there's plenty to read
and time to think
or i can just watch
machines fill

and sometimes
this slow laundry
is like
when i like
to make love to you

and now i stop
and kneel at
a washing machine window
like a voyeur
at the porthole
of our own orgasm
watching
my white seed
mixing with
your colorful petals
like a wildman
kissing flowers

## My Elbow Ancestry

i come
from a long line
of elbow users
my father
was one of the
bravest elbow drivers
in north america
swerving thru sundays
with free hands
and his floating
chicken wing
so sensitive
to the demands
of a sudden curve
and cheering children
his hands
would never
touch the wheel
and he would whip out
with his own gyrations
of elbow steering
long before
power steering
bopping back and forth
in a muscular ballet

till my mother
would cool him
with a "PLEASE ED"
and he would have to
save it
for the straightaways

and so if
my elbow
twitches into
your ribs
or rattles
the table
and spills
the coffee
it's nothing personal
just my father
on those ghost curves
still trying
to steer things
his own way


## As the World Turns

i saw you
peeking out thru the flower pots
and rattling the venetian blinds
for courage
stuck behind all your windows
you sucked at the glass
till your mouth finally bled
and you could stop
don't worry
everything is as it should be
the room
revolves around your waist
like the hoola hoop dream dance
for singles only

## Bunky Boy Bunky Boy Who's My Little Bunky Boy

i'll be going home today
to my mom and dad
and they'll sit me down
as if i've been sick
for a long time
or hypnotized unwell
and they'll feed me real good
to bring me back to my senses
and start telling me
what my old friends are doing
(at least the successful ones)
and i'll nod
sometimes applaud
cheer
i knew they could do it
wish them well
they must be happy
doing what they want
then everything will get quiet
and mysterious
my mother religious
will dim the lights
chanting entranced
will sacrifice a salami
quick and done
so her son may live
as a lawyer
or at least something
24 years old and nothing
how will she get to florida
and my father will be droning
eyes shut tight
presenting reality to me
in a secret handshake
and all I have to do
is accept it
a good life
and keep shaking so
he can forget about his

25 years of Food Fair Stores
25 years of bad lighting
fluorescent suns and electric doors
stolen green stamps
and christmas displays
25 years of coffee breaks
for what?
sugar diabetes and a no good son
his eyes still in the Depression
just trying to get ahead
but his practical goldwatch fingers
dreaming about designing handbags and hats
maybe a mistress
o if they could only make me suffer
and well
get for me
a good mortgage
a demanding wife
an immobile baby
make a person out of me
respect how hard they worked
so i could get smart
and make money
for them
and all the while
i'll be stirring my coffee patiently
born into debt
knowing they're desperate
and don't mean what they say
surely they love my poetry
respect my acting
have a great son
a different son
a real man
and i'll be stirring
in control
and my father will start whispering
Hitler again
and my gentile girl friend
The Loser
who will stab me in the back

eventually
and i'll be stirring
more and more frantically
in a berserk merry-go-round
splattering coffee over the refrigerator
the cabinets
my mother my father
it's what they wanted
and i've given in again
and right out the door i go
screaming at lampposts
crying on new cars
running from a posse
of lawn mowers
that will never let me escape
and where are the young girls
to see this
take me in comfort me
believe in me love me
where are the young boys
my friends from the basketball court
are they all locked up in College?
tomorrow the neighbors will be over
for breakfast
and they'll talk
and what stories of me!
they'll interview my mother
like a T.V. talk show
and she'll show them my poems
my pictures my letters
my sculptures my songs
and smile so proudly
to the camera

# John Newlove

## The Grass Is a Reasonable Colour

The world is composed
by the men who live in it,
singly, however dully.

This much is obvious: singly;
and whether it is wished
or detested

cannot be helped. The earth
of a sane man is sane,
must be. The flowers
are ordered as they must be,

the grass is green
in the proper seasons
and is cut in the proper seasons.
The trees bear orderly fruit.

The earth revolves
according to the calendar
and according to the calendar
the moon raises tides
in water and in women.

There is a time for anything.
Mistakes are explainable.

Things are as
they must be. In
the madman's world, I am told,

things are as they must be.
The earth revolves
according to a calendar.

The moon makes tides
in water and in men.
Mistakes are explainable.

The flowers are ordered.
The grass is a reasonable colour.
The trees bear fruit.


## Verigin, Moving in Alone

(fatherless, 250 people,
counting dogs and gophers
we would say, Jmaeff's grocerystore,
me in grade 4, mother
principal of the 2-building,
3-room, 12-grade school,)

a boy sitting on the grass
of a small hill, the hot fall,
speaking no russian, an airgun
my sister gave me making me envied.

I tried all fall, all spring
the next ominous year, to kill
a crow with it, secretly glad
I could not, the men
in winter shooting the town's
wild dogs, casually tossing
the quick-frozen barely-bleeding
head-shot corpses onto
the street-side snowbanks,

the highway crews cutting their way
through to open the road with what
I was sure was simply
some alternate of a golden summer's
wheat-threshing machine, children
running through the hard-tossed spray,
pretending war from the monster's snout,

leaping into snowbanks from
Peter The Lordly Verigin's
palace on the edge of town
in a wild 3-dimensional
cubistic game of cops and robbers,

cold spring swimming
in Dead Horse Creek and farmers'
dugouts and doomed fishing
in beastless ponds, strapped
in school for watching a fight,

coldly holding back tears
and digging for drunken father's
rum-bottle, he had finally
arrived, how I loved him,
loved him, love him, dead, still.

My mad old brother chased me
alone in the house with him
around and around
the small living room, airgun,
rifle in hand, silently,
our breaths coming together —

all sights and temperatures
and remembrances,
as a lost gull screams now
outside my window,
a 9-year-old's year-long
night and day in tiny
magnificent prairie Verigin:

the long grey cat we got,
the bruised knees, cut fingers,
nails in feet, far walks
to watch a horse's corpse
turn slowly and sweetly to bone,
white bone, and in the late spring,
too, I remember the bright
young bodies of the boys,

my friends and peers and enemies,
till everything breaks down.

## Verigin 3

The pure white bodies of my friends,
d'un blanc pur, like —
like a cigarette paper! shivering

in cold spring before a cold
shallow waterhole. Thin naked
bodies, ribs, knees, buttocks, hearts,

young bilingual doukhobors,
where are you now? I cut my foot
on a piece of rusty tin and walked home
alone, shoe full of blood.

## The First Time

When she put her hand on me
for the first time, the
first time, she whispered,
Let me hold it! Holy Jesus,

the first time! The man,
another one, a friend
of ours, snored lustily
in the drunken kitchen,

clothed under the pink blanket,
a nipple between my teeth,
finger in the wrinkled
cavity it was suddenly

my job to fill, I shuddered, I'm
too young for this I thought,
what will mother say? It's
so wet! Ah Jesus I can't.

But I could, and I had to, and
I did, from the first terrified
fumbling entrance to the
anticlimactic climax. And,

Oh, she said, oh that was
good, was it good for you?
And oh I said yes, trying to think
of anything else at all.


## The Well-Travelled Roadway

The dead beast, turned up
(brown fur on back and white
on the belly), lay on the roadway,
paws extended in the air.

It was beautiful on the well-travelled roadway,
with its dead black lips: God help me,
I did not even know what it was.
I had been walking into the city then,
early, with my own name in mind.

## Succubi

I don't dream anymore about arthritic spiders
hobbling knobbly-kneed across the floor
Or menstrual wheat! Or that long-tongued snake
running up my leg Black as Creation
dull sad water eyes like unpolished leather
Or dream-litter hitch-hiking descendants
all over the roadsides As if the crusts
of sons and daughters were as cheap as bread
All night I dream of Love and shoot the lovers dead
from the hip

I can go on inventing all night
But what I really dream
is those women suffocating me
their dead flesh denser than cold syrup to swim in
Slowing me down slowing me down

Dreams of the thick women turning
Turning and turning their gross bellies on me
wrapping their gelatin thighs and mottled breasts
Graving me deeper than winter mud Choking
with their red-grease kisses my airy mouth

They come down in the night
These women
sucking the very life out of me As lustful
themselves as my schemes are
and as cruel

# Alden Nowlan

## Beginning

From that they found most lovely, most abhorred,
my parents made me: I was born like sound
stroked from the fiddle to become the ward
of tunes played on the bear-trap and the hound.

Not one, but seven entrances they gave
each to the other, and he laid her down
the way the sun comes out. Oh, they were brave,
and then like looters in a burning town.

Their mouths left bruises, starting with the kiss
and ending with the proverb, where they stayed;
never in making was there brighter bliss,
followed by darker shame. Thus I was made.

## Gypsies

Jessie, my cousin, remembers there were gypsies
every spring, cat-eyes in smoky faces,
hair like black butter on leather laces.
Mothers on the high waggons whose babes sucked
flesh on O'Brien Street, I'd be ashamed.
The men stole everything and damned if they didn't
shrug if you caught them — giving back a hen
filched from your own coop like a gift to a peasant.
The little girls danced, their red skirts winking,
their legs were lovely, greasy as drumsticks.
And they kidnapped children. Oh, every child
hoped secretly to be stolen by gypsies.

## Waiting for Her

Waiting for her,
rain on the windshield,
cars passing,
their tires hissing
on the black pavement;

one minute the rain
pounding the car roof
as drummers
must have pounded
their drums at old executions,
with their fists,
not wanting to hear the screams;

the next minute so quiet
I can hear my cigarette
burning when I inhale.

I listen
for her, I know how
she walks at night
and in the rain, with a different rhythm.

I brace myself to pretend
if she comes I was sure she'd come,
if she doesn't that I don't care.


## Daisies

We walked a mile from the road and with every step
she broke off a daisy, till she held thousands
in a great bunch against her chest,

till they covered her face and her red-gold pigtails,
till the top of her head was the eye of a daisy;
she sniffed of them, tasted their petals and pulp,
felt their heads and stalks with her cheeks and fingers.

The soil was rich, had we walked all day
she could have kept counting her steps with daisies:
running back to the car she threw open her arms
and her body burst like a fountain of flowers.


## Therese

I tell Therese
I'd like to set fire
to all the haystacks,
just at dusk,
then sit on a hill and smell them burning.

I call that poetry.
But she smiles.
You'll never grow up, she says.

Then I tell her
about Dachau and Hiroshima,
although I think it blasphemy
to write poems
about pain not experienced,
and she says it frightens her
to talk of such things.
She has made me promise
we'll keep one friend
without intelligence
who'll drink tea in the kitchen and gossip.

She is a fool.
But she loves me
as we are asked
to love God:
without understanding.

Tonight, coming
to meet me,
she wore shorts
under a raincoat
and when she came near,
passing a street light,
with each step
I could see
her white thighs
glistening with rain.


## Party at Bannon Brook

At the dead end of a road twisting snakelike
as that out of Eden, in a hunting camp, the hoarse creek
    crawling
through the closed door like the wet ghost of some
    drowned Adam
coughing water on the floor, I sprawl on a straw-filled bunk
and drink rum with strangers:

        The chef in his tall white hat
        and apron embroidered
        with ribald slogans
        spears steaks with slivers
        of white pine, roaring.

Beside me in the leaping shadows
next the rough boards of the wall, her head
resting on a calendar from which all the months
have been ripped away, leaving only
the likeness of a woman
with orange skin and a body that might have been
stretched on a rack in the dungeons
of Gilles de Rais, it has such
unnatural proportions, a girl sits swaying
in time with the chef's song, her sweater
pulled out at the back, my circular arm
stroking the soft fat
of her belly — not because I love her

but because I am afraid.
             If we could do what we wish
I would tell them I understand:
this is the season
when the bobcat is not driven away
by smoke and the eagle
makes reconnaissance from the coast.

             But they would not listen.
             And they could do worse: tomorrow
             the chef will be cashiered, kill
                   eight hours
             sending bills to debtors and this girl
             address letters
             to the brains of dead men, each
                   a packaged pudding
             shelved in cold storage, and I

in whom despair
has bred superior cunning
will escape only by long study
of how the silver beads turn to gold, falling
by my employer's window, the icicles
stroked by an amorous sun.


**Porch**

Immersed in night, my senses sharpen, hear
the nervous splash of water that can't stop
falling but hesitates before each drop
breaks in a porcelain basin and the ear.

Moonlight flows through the oilcloth, a sheen
upon each grain of dust descending from
the fuliginous ceiling, platinum
stars woven in the windows like a screen.

Our bodies touch, each meeting separate:
her arm, distinct and compact, like a cat
soft on my shoulder, while both ankles strain
against mine, bone to bone, her drowsing breast
crowding me toward the wall, passion at rest —
and the dull pressure of beginning pain.


## Semi-Private Room

"Mr. Nowlan, are you asleep?"
In the morning he will waken me with his whistling.
He may even be singing when I open my eyes,
for he sings while the nurses cleanse his wound,
hums when they bathe him:
dance tunes of the 1920's and Scottish marches.
"Time to rise and shine, Mr. Nowlan!"
Now, in the orange darkness he is silently praying
that I don't hear his voice blurred by tears,
cracked from exertion,
praying the pillows sufficed
to muffle his sobbing.
"Mr. Nowlan, are you asleep?"


## A Psalm of Onan for Harp, Flute and Tambourine

When I was twelve I was kidnapped and sold as a slave
to the daughter of the Emperor:
I wore my hair long with a scarlet band across my forehead;
otherwise, I was perfectly naked except
for bracelets of gold on my ankles and wrists;
it was her whim
to hang little bells from my penis.
When she breakfasted
at a little Japanese table
facing a window
overlooking the sea,
it was my privilege to bring her
iced juice and grapes
and a single rose
on a silver tray.

When I was thirteen
I was permitted to kiss her feet.
Her cousins admired me.
The master of the kitchen
was careful not to bruise me.
When I carried
messages to her lovers
I wore sandals
made from Spanish leather.

When I was fourteen
I rode behind her
on a white mule
when she and her lover
sported with hounds and falcons.
Sometimes it pleased her
to have her wenches
play with me lewdly.

When I was fifteen
I was put to war;
and, being so brave and clever,
was made a freeman
and captain of a thousand.
When I was sixteen
I conquered a city.
When I was seventeen
the Emperor ennobled me.

When I was eighteen
I married his daughter.
Ah! How well I remember
how she cried out when
my sword of bone
plunged into her body,
how my hot seed scalded
her gasping thighs . . .

When I was nineteen
I became an Emperor.

## Kyran's Christening

I suppose it's because we're on foot I'm reminded
of a story by De Maupassant, the lot of us walking
toward the church with the baby in its christening gown,
not merely a group of persons together but a small
religious procession, in which nobody feels obliged
to put on a solemn face — that's half the beauty
of it, we laugh softly
out of kindness toward one another, it's still morning,
the sun is shining
on Kyran; her eyes aren't in focus yet,
I know that, if I didn't I might think she knew
more than was good for her, she looks so wise,
so pitilessly wise, and powerful for all
her tininess.
     I don't like the priest
who is bored, impatient and reads without expression;
I don't like his taking off
his vestments before we leave, tossing them over
the baptismal font.
        But I suppose he's
at home here, elsewhere it's the most infrequent
guest who is courteous even
to carpets and chairs,
         and, after all, he's not performing
for me but for his god
         whom one presumes will hear him
no matter how bad an actor
he may be.
    So Kyran Pittman
renounces the devil and all his works.
"Our baby," one of us calls her, and we laugh
softly because she isn't,
not really. When the salt is put in her mouth she doesn't cry.

# Robert Peterson

**Untitled Poem**

Hands folded like napkins in my lap
I'm staring willfully at my future.
A real good guy, bodily unobtrusive.
It's my teeth they're after.

Someone is trimming a hedge,
the Paris Express arrives . . .
It's the last lap at Le Mans, and the Band is playing,
What is the sound of one castanet, decaying?

Across my nose, the Dentist and Nurse speak in code:
"Are we cementing Mrs. Kershman's crown?"
"Have you seen the map?" "I'm going on a diet."

I can't nod. Even my beard is novocained.
Just concentrate on letting normal thoughts flow naturally.
She's built. Does she or doesn't she?


**At Veronica's**

Kate meets me at the top of the stairs,
            hides my name in her doll.
Puffing and wet, I say that is not my name at all.
            I'm Windy, which is why
I never wear a hat. She lets her family fall and runs
            to fetch water pistols,
Begging me not to shoot a thing
            except rain, or her toes.

Monica, an older mother, singing Irish lovesongs,
                    and the kettle on; Jason
Jolly in his pen, points to a young pinnacle
                    of tooth as if it were
The North Pole, and I a walrus, or a wish, or
                    an absent father.

The kettle boils. I end a smart jig, catch my breath,
                    drink my tea hot.
and my lovesong goes / I hum a mortal tune / and
                    am all and none of those.


**Untitled Poem**

A swim in Ohuira Bay:
ten strokes from pier to float,
twenty back.
Here the self is naked and wet

In this current
strategists and dreamers drown.
Keep one eye on Mexico
or forget it.

Water green as trees
and warm as bread,
fish rising to feed, all sorrows

At kissing level.
And overhead wild ducks soar like tracers
into forms as delicious as life or money.

**Highway Patrol Stops Me, Going Too Slow**

*One foot in front of the other, heel to toe*
*& walk like that . . .*

> But they don't say how far.
> Drink or Don't Drink,
> what's the difference? The mind
> continues to function harmoniously.
> At least they're not wearing helmets.

*Shut eyes, arms out from sides, move*
*finger of left hand to nose. Now*
*right hand to nose. Again . . .*

> Forbidden to navigate by the stars.
> I'm in here, gravity is out there.
> Don't look at the officers but
> around the officers. Lorenz, observing geese,
> called this the "triumph ceremony."

*Stand perfectly still on one foot.*
*Now on the other foot.*

> "We long for greater daring, greater risk,
> greater passion or folly in Peterson."
> Clacking storks, Brandy sequences.
> Burt Lancaster behind bars. Anchor chains,
> laser beams, old keys to catatonia.

*Now spread both arms out like a bird, lean back,*
*farther back — that's it, eyes shut . . .*

> Richard risking it all on nostalgia,
> Calvin airborne in a disconnected Mercedes,
> Mary's bad knee diagnosed as pure loneliness
> & other diehards working without a net. The sound
> of earth from space — one great moan.

*We're letting you go. A borderline case.*

Well, drunken Shriners got up like Arabs
ride camels to help crippled children.
I was looking for a little white line. But love
is circular. And isolated objects cease to exist.
Give it a free trial in the privacy
of your own home.


## For the Minority

*The King hungers for territory — therefore we fight.*
                                                    *Tu Fu*

Our objections to the war
are making the King angry
and his troops uneasy.

Not convinced
that those who have done us no harm
should starve and burn

We are suspected
of ulterior motives
by some subjects.

But to me merely unpopular
in an unpopular country
is no disgrace, and better that killing

Of official enemies
at lower levels
be done without pride or joy.

The National Purpose is said to be firm.
(Is said to be firm.)
But are we to fall in line grossly

Outside the Palace
without question
if the Flag is crooked?


196     *Robert Peterson*

When one is guided by conscience only
there is no other side
to which one can cross.

Even so, perhaps we no longer
belong here.


## The Groom's Lament

*After Ch'en Shih-Tao, of whom it was said: "In order to*
*obtain a good line, he will shut himself up in a room."*

Now that I've taken a wife,
farewell to those long nights
in the taverns!
No longer do I sit lighthearted
with wenches
or sad with friends
beyond sunrise; no longer
sleep crosseyed in my clothes.

Morning light on the mountain.
Soon I'll have forgotten
how to stagger.
But all this lovemaking!
I'm getting too old for it.


## Untitled Poem

In the 2 A.M. Club, a working man's bar,
waiting for a suit to be pressed
a desire to review all human emotions
is inspired by three beers.

Clever is the sun, seen through cold bourbon highballs.
Eternally undismayed are the pool shooters,
and greed is discovered in a sack of peanuts
not what it was a year ago.

The fear of being alone
can be eased
by thoughts of switches.

I am surrounded by unknown men
and my life to this moment
cannot be totally explained.


## Wingwalking in Oregon

Last Sunday petrified
on Bridal Veil, a beginner's climb,
trail no wider than a carton of Kents.
Nice cliff & Eiffel view
for families
fresh from church. But
goosed by heights, how can I
embrace the sublime
without a priest
& no goddam fence?

And now
Saddle Mountain,
called benign.
Trail this time
half a loaf of bread
& the scenery true
until I find
I'm looking over the edge
of Oregon
into the depths of Idaho,
potatoes, breadcrumbs, birds
& diseases of birds, starch in the blood,
playground donkeys, slides, songs
& other conveyances
of my childhood
& if somehow
I let go
& spider down

concentrated & green
what should I, if alive but above all
safe, remember, & to whom
will I complain?


## To Myself, Late, in a Myrtle Grove

Outside my cheap candle
festive lights & rumble
of a distant log-truck
nearer, loaded, down the canyon
solid as a boulder.

Steak & potatoes
seasoned with fingers
smelling of fish.

Bed scooped with a foot.
No moon. Beercan upside down
to the stars; to the ladies

Of Coquille
for this honest place
strong as a picnic table.

The night dark, close, & safe.
A clean river still running

And cows awake.

# David Phillips

**The Wave**

the wave rises, it falls
back
    into another thing
not a wave now
           disappears, as they say
leaves nothing

of itself is dead
if we mean the ocean
is living —

    I think of you
as you have been,
        yesterday or
some time last year
      we met, our memory
is correct to say
we had no existence
      before
that night
    in the other's eyes
there is no
forgetting

we've come back with
another wave
            to this shore
with no traces of
having been
            there, with nothing
even to lie
with nothing of other waves

waves we've loved in
                and cannot claim


**Old Storm**

father is hard to live with
something about failure at fifty
they all go through it

maybe like being lost
in some snow storm
and wolves and starvation
forcing you to eat
your own flesh

consuming
part by part

till nothing, even the heart
is left

but it's survival
and he's starving

to me
weathering storms
of my own making I
can sometimes hear myself

howling
long and loud
in the hunger
of his blizzard


## Words

she clasps a jewel
beneath her tongue

the embrace
of her words

beautiful
the wounds

perfectly
cut


## Fighting Her

fighting her

is like
trying to write
with a cigarette

burning in my mouth
words
an inward glow
fierce
the pain to speak

I suck smoke
out of my eyes

**Notes on a Long Evening**

send cards send
letters

God listens he says
lie quietly

the closest door
closes

behind your neck
a stirring

she laughs from
the page

the radio also
receives

her breasts sense
your eyes

the mail is late
today

time itself believes
you

she's not coming
ever

ever is a long
time

the radio plays 20 songs
an hour

God is a rabbit
with teeth

read Celine and
weep

read Celine and
laugh

write yourself
letters

keep the cards
coming

lock all the doors
tonight

expect
nothing


**Orange Juice Song**

well when you can't see the forest
and you can't see the trees

there's a problem
somewhere

I take down the last clean cup
pour orange juice into it

vitamin C
builds strong bones

good for the gums
soothes an aching heart

I write a song about orange juice

I can't see the greater scheme in all this
or the smaller schemes

last night we drank bourbon
it burned all the way down

soothes an aching heart that stuff
soothes just about anything else too

can't see the vitamin C in my orange juice
I've got a blind trust in brand names

I've got a blind brand in my heart
l-o-v-e love, I'm takin about

love baby
love is a forest of trees

if you think about it that way
bourbon and orange juice is a rotten way to get drunk


**Things of Late**

I'm eating alone lately
blue shows through the red curtains

I lie in the bath tub and watch
certain essentials present themselves

its the colour of an old kiss
I'm taking great pains with salads

I have two baths a day
I light candles which are blue

a literal fact
one bath at night with a good book

I recommend dry salami on rye
another in the morning

I turn on the taps with a certain reverence
the curtains are of porous burlap

this explains the sky showing through
nothing explains my eating alone

## The Lover to Himself

your love, love
in an old house, who
writes it down and
speaks

to closed tight
ears, who wakes
you when there's

no one and nothing
to disturb
such sleep

when there is
nothing
when you look
and nothing

when you turn away
it hurts
you say to love
like that, to end

an era of long stares
and words, its love
on a dull knife
to lie there

on your shadow, the one
that kisses back

# Marge Piercy

## 16/53

Your elephant adolescence in sandlots Brooklyn:
it sloshes like a washtub with nostalgia.
Heroes stalked in your attic dragging chains of words.
In the coalbin you lifted weights
your belly pink as strawberry icecream.
You counted your body hairs like daisies
foretelling love / notlove / notlove.
Pillows of snow, girls melted leaving damp rings.
At night you turned into a toad big as a gas storage tank
and brooded over Flatbush muttering warts
and curses imitated from your favorite books.
You lay in bed becoming snotgreen Dedalus:
you would not wash
wanting your Jewish mother to threaten you with rosaries,
excommunication, the hierarchic ashes of creaky saints.
In bed you were secretly thin with scorn
while your parents doted and tried to feed you
stuffed cabbage,
and outside the frowsy neighbors
eating their newspapers like grass and growing mad
with the cold dim light of television flickering in their eyes
danced, danced in the streets
for the burning to death
of Julius and Ethel Rosenberg.

## Hare in Winter

The wounded hare looks out
of the trap at me.
Animals rarely
force us
to meet their gaze.
How food stares.
Suddenly my tongue
floats in blood.

## I Awoke with the Room Cold

I awoke with the room cold and my cat
Arofa kneeding my belly.
I had been walking around the lower east side
while from every alley and fruit market and stoop,
out from under the ravaged cars,
the cats came running to me.
All the cats had heard I was moving to the country
because of my lungs
and they began to cough and sneeze and whine.
All the starving rat-gnawed rickety spavined cats
of the lower east side with their fleas and worms
and their siren of hunger
followed me through the teeming blocks.
They threw themselves under the wheels of trucks
in the effort to keep up.
They were rubbing my ankles and yowling
that I must take every one of them along.
They wanted to breathe air that was not stained.
They wanted to roll on wet grass.
They wanted to chase a bird that wasn't a dirty pigeon.
Then the demands of the cats were drowned out.
As I ran, all of the eleven and twelve and thirteen year olds
who had died of skag in the smoking summer
began to miaou and miaou and miaou
till all of New York was white with pain like snow.

## Nothing More Will Happen

You are rumpled like a sweater
smelling of burnt leaves and dried sea grasses.
Your smile belongs to an archaic boy of wasting stone.
You change shape like spilled mercury.
There is no part of you that touches me
not even your laugh catching like fur in your nose.
I am with you on a glacier,
white snowfield gouged with bluegreen crevasses.
There is no place to go.
We cannot lie down.
We blaze like a refinery on the ice.
Soon a dry snow will fall
in slow obliteration.
This death has an odor of gasoline.
Your hands fall to your sides.
Your eyes freeze to the rim of the sky.
Already I cannot see you for the snow.
The heavy iron gates
are closing in my breasts.


## Burying Blues for Janis

Your voice always whacked me right on the funny bone
of the great-hearted suffering bitch fantasy
that ruled me like a huge copper moon with its phases
until I could partially break free.
How could I help but cherish you for my bad dreams?
Your voice would grate right on the marrow-filled bone
that cooks up that rich stew of masochism where we swim
Woman is born to suffer, mistreated and cheated.
We are trained to that hothouse of exploitation.
Never do we feel so alive, so in character
as when we're walking the floor with the all night blues.
When some man not being there who's better gone
becomes a lack that swells up to a gaseous balloon
and flattens from us all thinking and sensing and purpose.
Oh, the downtrodden juicy longdrawn female blues:
you throbbed up there with your face slightly swollen

and your barbed hair flying energized and poured it out,
the blast of a furnace of which the whole life is the fuel.
You embodied that good done-in mama who gives and gives
like a fountain of boozy chicken soup to a ratrace of men.
You embodied the pain hugged to the breasts like a baby.
You embodied the beautiful blowsy gum of passivity,
woman on her back to the world endlessly
    hopelessly raggedly
offering a brave front to be fucked.
That willingness to hang on the meathook and call it love,
that need for loving like a screaming hollow in the soul,
that's the drug that hangs us and drags us down
deadly as the icy sleet of skag that froze your blood.


## Kneeling Here, I Feel Good

Sand: the crystalline children
of dead mountains.
Little quartz worlds
rubbed by the wind.
Compost: rich as memory,
the visible castings of our pleasures,
orange rinds and roses and beef bones,
coffee and cork and dead lettuce,
the trimmings of hair and lawn.
I marry you, I marry you.
In your mingling under my grubby fingernails
I touch the seeds of what will be.
Revolution and germination
are mysteries of birth
without which many
are born to starve.
I am kneeling and planting.
I am making fertile.
I am putting
some of myself
back in the soil.
Soon enough
sweet black mother of our food
you will have the rest.

## Someplace Else

Blackberries sweet and dusty.
Our hands are stained a sticky purple
as we walk roads that crawl tentatively
among the ponds, puddles, inlets and pools.
The sea is wearing through the soil.
The island floats like a coarse net.
Elderberry blossom. Broom. Beach plum.
Bees are shaggy with pollen.
Their honey is good.
Here wood is weathered and damp.
Fog pours like milk over the hills.
Nothing is visible from the highest hill
but the sea.
The plovers and sandpipers are not afraid of us
making love on warm sand beside a grey log.
Your body and mine smell like the sea.
Every while we must run away to be healed,
three days, a day, half a day running to landscapes
where birds outnumber people
hidden from the sounds of the war we live.
We are harmless here
and the place rolls over us like the evening fog.
Seven years, and every day crowds us out of each other
stripped like gears with hard use.
We are the real island we escape to, briefly,
in the sea that is salty like our blood.


## Councils

We must sit down
and reason together.
We must sit down:
men standing want to hold forth.
They rain down upon bowed heads
and faces lifted.
We must sit down on the floor
on the ground
on the earth

on stones and mats and blankets.
There must be no front to the speaking
no platform, no rostrum,
no stage or table.
We will not crane
to see who is speaking.
Perhaps we should sit in the dark.
In the dark we could utter our feelings.
In the dark we could propose
and describe and suggest.
In the dark we could not see who speaks
and only the words
would say what we think they say.
No one would speak more than twice.
No one would speak less than once.
Thus saying what we feel and what we want,
what we fear for ourselves and each other
into the dark, perhaps we could begin
to begin to listen.
Perhaps we should talk in groups
the size of new families,
not more, never more than twenty.
Perhaps we should start by speaking softly.
The women must learn to dare to speak.
The men must learn to bother to listen.
The women must learn to say I think this is so.
The men must learn to stop dancing solos on the ceiling.
After each speaks, he or she
shall say a ritual phrase:
It is not I who speak but the wind.
Wind blows through me.
Long after me, is the wind.

## Unclench Yourself

Open, love,
I tell you we are able
now and then gently
with hands and feet
cold even as fish
to curl into a tangle
and grow a single hide,
slowly to unknit all other skin
and rest in flesh
entire.
Come all the way in, love,
it is a river
with a strong current
but its brown waters
will not drown you.
Let go.
Do not hold out
your head.
The currents know the bottom
better than your feet.
You will find
that in this river
you can breathe
and under water see
small gardens and bright fish
too tender
for the air.

# J. D. Reed

**The Gorilla at Twenty Nine Years**

*Only by looking at gorillas as living, feeling beings was I
able to enter into the life of the group with comprehension,
instead of remaining an ignorant spectator.*
George Schaller, The Year of the Gorilla.

Twenty nine years of stale cake and flat ale,
of the gorilla mouth belching bamboo shoots,
young and tender; twenty nine of moderate thought:
I expected a change of heart, at least of mine,
but iron frying pans clash on my ears,
a dime drops through the machine endlessly.
I can barely count to ten.

This is not the truth?
I want to hear one nursery rhyme
over and over a thousand times
until the syllables shatter
into Rumpelstiltskin's gibber:
a gorilla with a prize in oratory.

Ten years of working at it,
never quite went over the edge
of the abyss; I dangled,
a one-lunged arachnid on a thread

of twenties, a Detroit bankroll,
and clanged my garbage lids of "style."

Ten times I said, "my heart is chrome"
in lying notebooks. What I meant was "mirror."
Ten years of distrust, ten of hybrid scholastics;
in and out of schools like a heartbeat,
boring as a pulse. Ten of false selflessness.

For five years the heart knew
it could be exchanged for one of elastic,
a sock-foot beating in the chest.
Five years were free inside a bottle, *perepeteia*,
lashed like a waxed gorilla to vodka's mast.
The urinals sang five songs,
I strained at the five ropes of my fear.
A note propped on the mantle by the ship
in the bottle: she won't be back.

Five years dumb-tongued,
lax and sterile. Five of nest building,
a succession of gorilla butts I pressed to
pretending sleep or love. Five years
of women forgiving. Bless them,
fur and all.

One year of knowing I lived
through lives of other men,
knowing it's not right & wrong,
not process-product, or ball bearings
clicking in equal and opposite reactions,
not gorilla options in a laboratory.
One year of finding no principle
                    in uncertainty,
a year of drawing the spear blade
half-way out to see if the tip is poisoned,
a cross-section of the dance.

This day the gorilla polled his friends:
they showed the tartar on their teeth,
scratched and grinned.


**Cripples**

The ones who hammer the air with fists
or ones with moving lips, trying to repeat
the soundless instructions of physical therapists,
or the boy with saliva on his yarmulke

chanting geometric theorems, or the veteran
in the electric wheelchair, rubber tires
squeaking over tile, muttering, "cathode, diode,"
or the girl, one puckered leg clicking in its brace,
a hobbled chemistry of sties and baths at night,
flounces the reducible fraction of her sexuality
like a petticoat: o moon droolers,
o hairlips pooping speech. O men and women.


## Stony Brook Tavern

And the first among them
would be Tom Foley, Irish-
man and damned sinner
with the rest of us,
peers wise-puppy-wise
over the bar's back side:
a gentleman and rogue.

He gauges his drinks,
tight as a hawser;
goes home each afternoon
as if from sea,
where thirty years
went under a tanker's keel.

He stood before a soft coal oven
as if it were the Dublin symphony;
fried steaks in sea's pitch
and watched the forbidden whiskey roll
in a chain-locker nightcap.
He pilots this tavern
as if it steamed up a port channel.

Foley on his duckboard bridge
dreams nights gone under Galveston's
plowed surf; grease, black griddles,
port and sweet muscatel: sticky Gulf nightmares

so bad when he woke on a whore's bed,
flies spelled his name on the screendoor.
Dream of bare bulb rooms,
and lime burns in plaster d.t.'s.

In Boston's hospital
for the seaman's liver,
he shook poached eggs on the gown,
remembered Aqua Velva passed
through a loaf and drunk
in the galley hatchway.

Now pisseyed in the afternoon
of trucker's arguments,
anchored on this gravel sea of parking lot,
he stands at the taps dreaming
Rahway and oil slicks.
Visions of priests and world-wise mates
fill him like a bilge. He loves
salt, itself.


**Out from Lobster Cove**

All day swaying in the tower
forty feet from deck,
*beat hell out of it,*
    *Beautiful Thing.*
White caps are cotton a nurse uses
to swab out this boil of ocean.

One man, one vote, one thing
stretched and cut . . .
deaf to whole numbers
in the false wind of sixteen knots,
I look for the white bloat
of tuna belly turning on a mackerel.
    What matters to me
I tear from the book and save:

part of a ticket, my father's
Mason's ring, thirty seconds
over Tokyo.

    I see tops of heads
on the bridge, see from up here
that the blind must think with their eyes,
that the amputee loves me
with his pear-wood limb; that the dead,
the dead they live on the worms
in their lovely parts.

Boom swings full tilt inboard,
block of ice (300 lbs.) splinters
on the hatch cover.
    A tendon swells
and throbs.

He got way up the hill
in his Merc, popped the clutch
and almost smelled rubber
when the wheels left the dock.
His sleeping mistress slept on,
he went
              that far out.

Abeam of the swell,
the main bearing's a flounder brain
in the black guts of the engine.
Roll with it,
jelly-knee in the lookout.
Your brown arm throws a bottle leeward.

On board eight miles off Folly Point
you can't say this
is where I get off. No,
you're here all day,
    *beat hell out of it.*

Running across the bay,
salt caked on the binnacle,
I steered all night at 345°, or just off that;
my dirt-bred hands tight on the wheel,
until York Harbor's lights
clicked off at dawn, and I throttled back
into a channel once more.

See it skim the water out from Maine!
Hear it buzz, please, and thump on a short chop —
this new speedboat loaded with men and girls.
Far from this perch, binoculars are like a movie
you make up from parts of things.

Tuna:
    we angle in from their port,
Gayhead harpooner balanced in the pulpit,
switch off and glide
    into their school.
He hefts the ash lance with its double head.
    It must enter
just behind where the ear would be.
It makes a boomerang, half in
and half out of water.

The black back rolls,
line sings around a fin
and the keg goes over, hollow.
He'll drag himself to death this way:
the dart working in toward his parts.

Where I went, I went in fits,
*beat hell out of it,*
and went stooped over
without sea-charts.
Where I went with my flesh
was my business, I forget.
I picked up the Joads out there,
hugged the lightning and kissed

the bride's sweet knee. I sulked
and moved at night. I forget.
    *Beautiful Thing.*

Forty feet from the blade,
forty from the belly gouge,
I can't go down to drink
the blood from a cup,
we're after two.

I keep a level eye for surface signs:
a hump, a fin, a tail,
any part of flesh alive breaking water.
We hack at the parts we see,
trusting this space we live in.

The cracks in the windows filled,
the brine bubbled in,
his breath went out and stopped.
His wallet floated up around his eyes,
and butts swam from the ashtray.

He went out to the end of the dock,
to see what he could see:
part of the tugboat tied
to part of the dock. Part of the water
lapping both, o, cone of light!
holystone,
    *beat hell out of it,*
yellow soap and brass polish.
We wash parts from the deck,
skin and blood we couldn't use.

The liver soaks in brine, a few red steaks
fry in the galley. White fish
on a blue field, our tuna pennant rips the air.
One thing is done, and it bells
up in the throat.

# Dennis Saleh

**The Thumb**

To end it all, the people elected a thumb.

It stood before them blankly,
as a thumb would.

Its nail flickered and blinked
in the fires people put at its feet
at night.

The people would sit with it,
holding each other, rocking.

It was strange.

What was the meaning of the cloud
joined neatly to the cuticle.
What was the cuticle doing.

Like a leader,
the thumb stood in mystery.

And what did it do? What could it do.
It pressed.

Like an iron, a tack,
like the pages of a book coming together
for the last time.

## The Furniture of the Poem

I'm driving my car back to you filled
with the furniture of this poem.
I have everything here,
even the school I screwed you behind.

In the glove compartment, what I
remembered of your hair. Right next to me,
your sweaters, a pack of cigarettes,
some lipstick. Look, in the ashtray,

your eyes. I've got your girdle stretched
over the steering wheel. Your earrings
dangle from the mirror. Thoughts of you
are everywhere. I'm really moving now.

I have your car in my trunk. I'm sitting
on your Father. Your Mother's in the
back seat looking for you. As I pull up
in front of your house, your bed crashes

off of the hood. The neighbors are coming.
I'm jumping out, see? Look, I have
your clothes. You're probably naked.
Don't be afraid, Here I am, Here I am!

## Nesting

This is everyone's marriage.
Everyone's all lined up.
The men are over here. The women here.
I take my place not exactly
anywhere.

We begin marching.
We're all trying to keep up.
We're thinking of all that furniture,
the responsibilities.
All the lovely parts of our bodies.

Pretty soon we get there.
Now the young marrieds
find their almond trees.
We all climb up into them.
Someone says, "Something should be said."

I suggest something
about the loveliness of the trees,
how fortunate we are
to tuck in among
the grey and green fur of the almonds.

Everyone is afraid to begin.
We all blush. Someone says,
"Something should be said."
No one clears their throat.
No one says anything.

We hang in our trees like moons,
our reflections
falling around us in a rain.

But the morning is better.
In the morning we climb down from all this,
slow, determined,
our gaze
fixed like something about to be born.


**Inventing a Family**

*from*

**A Guide to Familiar American Incest**

You can have daughters, sons.
Parents, if you like. An uncle or aunt.
All the relations, all in your home.

Point, and your knee is a son,
white, knobby.
He'll follow you. You'll name him.
Just reach down. He's there.
You can hug him. Never be alone.

Across the room imagine a wife.
Stretch her out on the couch.
Put her there, on the couch, like a friend.

Have as many daughters
as you can. Delight in them.
See them as women, grown.
See them as nothing like your knee.
They are your stomach, or your hands.

Have a father, have a mother.
Have anniversaries.
Trouble yourself remembering birthdays,
the seasons moving through your rooms.

Soon you'll never be alone.
Imagine that.
Sitting together. Eating. Talk
in the dark.
Whole rooms full.
Arrange whole nights up.
Everyone talking to everyone.
Father to Mother. Brother to Sister.

Your knees. Your stomach.
Feel so much stirring. Feel yourself.
Never be alone. Never be alone.
Turn over in the dark. Careful.
There's Mother. There's Sister.


**The Bed**

One day
two people decide to build a bed
and sleep the rest of their lives together
in it.

They gather quantities of wood, metal, cotton.
Soon they are tufting a mattress,
fashioning springs.
Chips and scraps pile at their feet.

The bed grows, like a family.
The two people take an unmistakable pride
in what they are doing.
They reach across the bed, touching.

Several days pass without sleep and the people
continue working.
The bed is grander than they expected,
stretching between them like a city.

The two people break from their work frequently,
to smile at each other,
but soon days pass at both ends of the bed
without a word spoken.

The work is exhausting, and lonely.
The work stops.
One of the two people carves into the headboard,
"I hate you."

The room the people are in softens,
out of a respect for the present, or the future,
and tries to heal the scar,
or heal over the bed.

But nothing heals, and the two people stand
like the boundaries of a city,
neither city, nor not the city,
but what makes the city what it is.


**Story**

*The Mother*

wished to have been milk,
to have passed out of herself entirely,
to have passed out of her nipple.

She searches through herself
for the devil's mark,
the place her son can enter
and not be felt.

Oh if she finds it

*The Son*

behaves peculiarly,
as if sensing what will fall
to him to do.

If he stands at a window,
he tastes it. His tongue reaches out
hesitantly to touch the glass,
half expecting to press through it
to nothing.

When he passes them,
he is afraid he will press
through his mother,
press through his sister.

He watches his father as though
watching a manta ray
approach him from a closet.

*The Daughter*

lingers in the bathroom.

She stands on the scale
and imagines how the years
will touch her here, and so,
delicately, like a towel.

Her breath is short, heavy,
a whisper that grows between her legs
like grass to be cut
late in the morning, when dry.

## The Father

Everything he says catches
in the air before him,
is a pale and wobbly reflection
nodding gently from his mouth.

He follows it from room to room,
and it crosses and re-crosses
the balloons he sees in everything,
the tense balls of promise.

The father is nothing exacting,
only the suggestion of water moving
through water, parting water.

## The Penis

It should be porcelain
and harmless. Or we should
be able to warm our hands at it.

It could warm our hearts.

It will make the air in the room
ring like a bell
and it will beat for an answer.


## The Return

I sit in a huge auditorium
behind my father.
I see his ears and study the neck,
the folds there,
like creases of earth,
I watch the grey hair soften
in the still air.
In front of him is his father,
and more fathers, stretching
down in a single row.

227     Dennis Saleh

While I am counting the fathers,
my father's eyes roll back into
his head and lock on mine.
They stare into me past his brain,
through all the flesh he has managed
and managed to grow for years.
There are eyes staring into him,
eyes staring up
from the dark of the hall.
All the hair is grey,
all the hair is dying,
the eyes say climb down
over the seats, into your father.
All the fathers calling their sons
climb down,
into the hair, save the dying hair,
smooth the creased earth,
kiss the neck.
I stand and don't think.
I touch the father in front of me,
he touches a father,
I climb over the seat.
The hall stirs with all the light
that has gone.
From behind something is rising,
my eyes roll back,
I open my mouth and open my mouth,
like a mouth
yawning and never closing.

# Tom Schmidt

**Butter**

Today at the Gateway
to the Pacific
Travis AFB California
we loaded a cattle
truck full with
bodies fresh off
the plane from Con Thien.

Vacuum sealed in
smooth extrusions as
shiny and neat
as your latest poptop
beer can:
> Container, Cadaver
> Aluminum, PROS 1467, Reusable
>
> Nomenclature of Contents:
> The human remains of
> Transportation # 757XOD3967 Cpl E4

(or some kind
of sergeant once
that weighed 43 lbs net.)

Tarp over to protect
motorists from the glare
on the highway
to Oakland the truck
pulled out and we watched
silent
    wiping wet palms
on our green thighs.

## Seven Mexican Children

I saw them at games every
day, down the jungle hill from the
hotel they moved in the shiny
leaf like butterflies through
green fog. An afternoon I

returned from the tepid bay to find
them squatted by the road in
the shade of a brown wall. I
approached and they fluttered, seven

rows of brilliant teeth
blazing out of half darkness.
Beside their circle I saw
they'd caught a bat and crucified

him there, the awful boney
wings and one crusted foot pronged
in the dirt with three small twigs.
He twisted his mouse's head

and bleeped as a beautiful little
girl tried inserting a coffee bean
between his needle fangs.
The free foot clawed the air
valiantly, but when he seized and
coughed a streak of stringy blood down
his chin we all knew.
I stood till a cloud of

infinitely small lice deserting
the depleted host turned
all the red earth around him black and
the bleeps began to go away.

Children turned to smile once more, I walked
on up the hill to the hotel.
When I stopped at the bar to
test a shot of tequila my sandaled
feet began to itch.

230    Tom Schmidt

**Butcherboy**

Late Saturday afternoons in Emeryville
where it's all black now
I rolled paper, the old kind
color of Pepto-Bismol,
over the display case windows.

Dad turned off the chicken singeing flame.
I took the meats out of the case on trays.
Inside the walkin box he snatched headcheese
when I passed, his sandwich,
he opened up the mustard, a pint of Coreys.
I got out the black rubber hose. He spread
the mustard. I sprayed the week's crud,
the particles of meat stuck on the glass.
He ate his sandwich, yellow rings on his lip,
the bottle. I wiped the slicer. He took off
his apron with flowers of blood, talked about
Yank Yankovich, the polka. I scraped
the chopping block, the rows of teeth
under my hand chewing out balls of fat and blood.

He put on his hat. I swept the old sawdust.
He went home to change. I spread the new sawdust.
I cleaned the grinder the tenderizer
and all the knives. He danced the polka.

Seventeen, cleaning the knives, I cut off the thumb
of my left hand. These knives are sharp,
I thought to myself, holding my wilting hand
over my head like a flaming torch. A lady clerk
in the grocery department fainted. I put my
thumb in the tallow bin. Somebody called the ambulance.

I was 4F and it doesn't really get in my way
unless I wanted to work in a butcher shop.

## Drowning in Spanish

If you are
in Spain,
drowning going

down the third
time and yell
*ayudame!*
which means
help!
the people will
think except in
Spanish of
course help?

what does he mean
help?
      Because
for drowning they
say *auxilio*
which means
aid

Try that
at Stinson
Beach


## A Long Overdue Thankyou Note to the
## Girl Who Taught Me Loving

Visiting home to tell my people
the latest girl I love, real this
time, I thought one morning of
the girl who taught me loving.
Both fifteen years old, she already
beautiful and kind, fine
olive skin, hair so black I used
to swoon from just one smell of
it and still yes a bit coltish;

me such a dummie I can't forget.
But once standing by a tree some-
where I somehow said something
to make her lower her eyes, smile,
take my hand saying, Oh Tom, Oh.
We held for one breath while I
hoped forever because just then
I knew love was more than sweaty
adolescent strokings and things
we learned from dirty jokes. I
kissed her, knowing lips at last,
clashings of teeth set aside. A
long time has passed. I heard
she is years older than I now with
her lots of kids and tired husband.
Dear Adele, do tell me, is love
long enough?

Even as I sat on the
porch sketching this
poem my old mother
came out with the
kitchen mop to shake —
Remember Adele Cortese,
mom? I said. She said,
Why'd you *always* have
to fall for those
darkies? Gave the mop
a snap, went inside.
I guess, like they say,
If she has to ask she'll never
know.

## Civilization

The sound of water running
does something to cats.
I shave, or pee,
I take a shower
and they gather at the door

like anthropologists,
their eyes clear and scientific
but puzzled,
looking for breathing grasslands,
thirst, the wild hart

turning his pretty eyes
to a pool in shadows,
nose taken by the immediate scent
of water
as he dips
his brown head

to drink.

## In the Garden

On my knees
thinning the spinach
I hear heavy sighing
behind me.
It's Emerson in the potatoes,
filling his pail.

I refrain from asking:
What are you doing in there?
A bouquet of spinach
in my fist like a pledge
I stand and walk toward him, saying:
But those Russets aren't ready yet!

His mouth opens.
Instead of words his breath
reaches me across the garden,
the spinach rustling
in the wind of his Spirit,
green flags

before a rainstorm.
When the wind subsides
he is gone but for
his half-filled pail
and Yankee coat on the ground
turned inside out
like a dirty stocking.

If you asked me a week ago
I'd have told you
Emerson's the last famous poet
I thought I'd ever meet.


## The Creeper

Strange creeper
rushing silent greens
down a corner
of our house ignored

until prying at the window
it threatens interrupting
one of my dreams.

I decide to cut the creeper
move in to its cold shadow
with rusty clippers

and sorry guts.
Pollen flies I choke
the creeper snares at my
ankles my wrists I pull

a severed mass stinking
away from the wall.
The creeper has been
smothering a spindly peach tree

against the wall the peach tree
freaked for survival has been
vining out for the sun whirling

fuzzy shoots out creeping
the creeper pretending to be all
it is not. I begin hacking

at the peach tree the vines the
creeper the vines
and the vines and
I stop. I wade thru

the cuttings
they cling along until I am
knee deep in wet stinking
cut creepers in the middle

of the yard.
I extricate myself
carefully go back

to the naked fragile
peach tree vine-sapling and
cut the remaining stragglers.

Three leaves remain the tree will
survive. I rake the mess
the vines I rake
the vines.

**Black and White**

Holstein cows parked
in the pasture by my house
in the suburbs

I can't stand it
chewing chewing so stupid

One foggy day after 6 months
looking at them
took 5 old 78 records
      Joe Venuti
      Bing Crosby
      Jimmy Dorsey
      Bob Scobey
      Jack Martini
walked out in the pasture
in the middle of the Holstein cows

Flung those thin discs
black moons
against the white sky

I call it
Giant Juggling
you hustle to lay all the wax
on the wind at once

No one there
but me and the Holsteins
the discs knifing
edgewise in the soft pasture ground
a hit parade landscape

I threw them again and again
up and down
back and forth
to fetch them
till the cows come home

That's all

237     Tom Schmidt

# John Oliver Simon

**6**

the cities are washed into time
the riders begin
to reclaim the territory
block by block,

in a shadow of myself
I pass thru matching
pigs boudoirs with barbed wire & crocodiles
eating each other under the pale skin
of a violet lagoon

I was there
wandered into the next room
and you didnt know I'd ever been born
hands still
tied behind my back

found a dead moth in the
pages of lamentations

being american we were
born without this knowledge.

## A Tryptych for Jan Bockelson

*"those wishing to consider the scenario of rebellion check
out Munster, Germany 1534-35 (Cohn, Pursuit of the
Millennium, Harper Torchbooks) where armed communists
proclaimed free love & the abolition of money & held off the
Bishop's troops for 15 months. might have won but the
honcho turned stalin instead of resolutely pursuing the
retreating enemy. they were all massacred & nothing
came of it."*

1

armed we go. we are the dancers
traipsing to armageddonon the new hiway

it felt so good to stop the traffic. swagger
like a mounted cop
with the streets in our hands

trample down haythorn, buckthorn whatever
scratches out our eyes

& her fingers in my hair were the
feet of deer in the liveoak

2

the man kept blowing that damn tin bugle
on the 3rd stroke of doom the
king was supposed to
rise up & there was
going to be a revolution
all over Germany

the man's face fragile & shaking a tin badge
dangling from his buckskin jacket a
bulge in his pants & a thin
beard near
sighted look the sun a tin
dazzle.

trumpeter of the new jerusalem
come out come out wherever you are
shouting to the unseen
archangels & dominations of the end
of history & all of us
had to go out in the square & the king would
lead us out women children & all
against the soldiers

then
he explained he only meant it all in a
spiritual sense
so we went back home
I remember we saw the
trumpeter pissing against a gray
stone wall in the
street of the archangel michael
melted a yellow trickle in the snow

3

masked

& you cannot tell the ending of one from another
their
fingers merge into one tangle full of leaves.

these men who held the city fifteen
        months for an idea
the king is the person of the state.
that was not it, the idea
many reforms that were put into practice

running to & fro in streets & into shadow
passageways, a man
blowing a bugle
the dead rise up from their boxes & cross the great
water

sun splashing without fault on stone buildings
bombardment broken
sometimes we have these heroic ideas
a picture of the heavens opening, armed love

who was it made the war & who let the innocent
children starve in no mans land
between the lines
why was there no revolution
for a thousand years.
I demand

the masked men are a spangle of leaves in the
suns crown


## Dont Tell Bad Dreams Says Tita's Mother

in the violet country
        of the knights of pentacles
                late summer blond wild grass.
we shot down
        a plane 8 inches long.

someone had to be notified
        the knight was staring at his own
                face in a mirror
i mean at my face
        in a mirror face
of the earth
                and the sun was sad too

we were afraid
to talk to the jovial
        people on the phone. this
                came true when the FBI
visited the shop today asking about
        weird david

why do i worry about those
        fuckin rednecks in the dream
                with shotguns i saw crawling
        thru the waisthigh yellow
grass when i was looking
        in the mirror


## The Woodchuck Who Lives on Top of Mt. Ritter

the woodchuck who lives on top of Mt. Ritter
dont take shit from nobody
you might see the golden
brown of him lying close down on the black
talus. you might see him scamp across the rocks

he lives on raisins, bread, sardines, chocolate
climbers leave — 7 parties made the top for instance
sunday 19 july 1970. every now and then
a gaggle of sierra clubbers with brand new ice axes
maybe 45 of them. this means a feast. weekdays
he might get some grubs, airborne spores
of trout — trout must have airborne spores
or they wouldn't be in Nydiver Lake
above Shadow Falls. who knows, weekdays
maybe he works the camps on Lake Ediza
but how does he get up & down the glacier.

the woodchuck, i think he is a woodchuck.
he lies in air & is cautious.
13 thousand feet of air
black rocks color of electricity
his throat is flattened against the
stone, watching me
dark eyes as those of us who came from water

his fur
on his front haunches rises & ripples
soft as yellow grass in the late
wind. his back same golden under
hair-backs brown as earth. now he's
coming around a corner,
eaten the bit of bread i
threw him. nostrils
gray quivering
if he cares he can
see Mt. Goddard, the Clark Range, hazy golden
rock and torn with snow beneath thunderheads.
ah woodchuck

does he have a wife, is he raising babies
to follow his trade — next summer, my son
the summit of Banner will be yours.
when it thunders he waits
gently in talus caverns
far from danger, possibly with their soft bodies
leaning around him

the man who sees him goes downhill from this
phantasmic beast among incredible
colors, white snowbell cassiope, indian
paintbrush red with yellow spikes, the
purple and yellow he has no names, his
hands the earth the clouds the air the evening
star a black mountain
shoulder rising to catch it
his face does not see all the colors

the woodchuck who lives on top of Mt. Ritter
is very careful and shows himself
only to those who come quiet and
with no intention to harm.
somebody has to
do what he is doing
because the waste from human
people must be consumed & changed into
gravity meadow grass stars insects & baby woodchucks.
i didn't write this in the summit register
for fear somebody would come from
Washington to check the woodchuck's headlights
and make him pay his income tax.
or rip off his mountain in the timehonored
tradition of what they are trying
to do to the universe

**For Alan Blanchard**

today between skirmishes
I saw nutmeg & oranges in a rare
light

dispersed thru the sewers this
morning. blind with green strobes
touching the way,
my helmet in my hand

al lying blinded within
the perimeter of the national guard.

guard truck shuddering 6 feet
over my head in the black
noon
the only man passing free
between oxford and grove.

annabel lee on the radio
oranges and bright leaves
closing the doors of the sun.

## Living in The Boneyard

lime condensed on the ceiling, or maybe
yellow

      spider eggs
          X in yellow chalk where pete tried to
             mark the rain,
        last winter

      but it gets in anyway
           got to use inkrags to soak it
           up


      this might be termed living in the boneyard.

a golden lion of judah

    grins out of the menorah

        I never lit this year.

    next to my elbow the sea is

        full of dying birds

    suck up their curses & breathe on me
          again boys, it's

    a long way to the end of the world but if

        you let your breath out slowly in the

    middle of the first
        line maybe no one
will notice

# Stephen Vincent

## The Relationship

To be married,
to be a simple, smooth, loving thing:
that's what I wanted,
that's what I wanted.
But I could not give it to her,
no, I could not.
For me she would break apples,
make toasted cheese sandwiches,
with thin slices of bacon,
and put paprika in the tea.
We would wake up at three;
I would get the oranges
she bought with thick skins,
and she would peel them
with a paring knife
and we would sit and make love
and eat them piece by piece.

Day and night she was with me.
Quiet or with or without talk.
In the day we would walk through the City park
and walk on our hands or crawl on our bellies
to tell the colors of the winter leaves.
In the evening as the sun went down,
we climbed stair-wells to look at chimney pots
and see them in their different child-like shapes
and I would recount what they had in common
with our, what I called, relationship.

And in the evening we would return
to our secret backyard flat and tell each other
favorite children stories that we thought
we knew the best until it came time
for us to get undressed. And this we did
week after week with hardly a pause
in this our merriment. Only once or twice
did she call me coward, pull the mustard
off the shelf and bloop it through the air /
curling the stuff around my head & throat.
                                    But I got her back,
you can bet, when she had to clean
the yellowed shirt.

Yet somehow it happened, I do not know why,
it came time to leave her from that
our backyard flat. Oranges, tea and sandwiches,
I could not give it back. She said it was my mother,
but I would not give into that. And leave her,
yes I did, yes I did and yes I do, yes I do
regret the loss of her felicity,
                    the talk of marriage, children
and the lot. And in the evenings, you can bet,
I climb City stair-wells and sing this my song
to unmarried and single
chimney pots.


**Jealousy**

Go friendly, Go lovely, Go naked
My songs: the morning
Is for breathing. If you meet Eric
Tell him to get undressed. If you meet
Elizabeth, tell her I love her
And to get undressed. If you meet them
Together, help them get in bed:
Encourage their love and sleep,
And, if they ask of me, say
There is nothing between us.

## Coming Up & Falling Down

You were brought up
on the edge of that bay. Boats, fish,
the sky, the moon,
you had your way
into all of them. You could stab bass
off the end of the ferry pier
(your daddy the time-keeper)
and flip them back
into your ol' lady's frying pan.
Everything was that close. Crystal sets,
model planes, houses, you were the
skinny Okie with hot nuts
to build everything. Already
a third boat by my birth.
How come it all had to come back down
in such a terrible way? Is it
because you lost and broke your plane
in a national contest
taking you back to Detroit
when you were only fourteen?
Or was it your father's hobble?
Come on. Let's go. I want an answer.


## Basketball

I never let you come to the games. I never
invited you. You never asked. You never
saw me on the court handle the round skin
of the basketball. You never came to see me
spread my warm fingers like the edges of stars
around the ball as I went like a smooth fox
down the court my tennis shoes squeaking faster
than a grasshopper through clover. At sixteen
I travelled fast
father. Lay in, set shot, jump shot, bounce pass,
chest pass, bucking, elbowing as high as I could,
reacher for what was never given, the smooth flow
of the ball arching high towards the rim, its high arc

lifting subtly down, a smooth swish through
the star shapes of the unbroken
white net. Let me play that game again. I was on the court
with Willie, Leroy, Hobo & Sam. I the only white
with four blacks. Don't get me wrong. I was scared of them
as you of me or I of you. But it began. Somebody
poked me in the eye, it stung, and I released everything
travelling up and down the court a young man
with a quick gun and a sharp elbow. For the first time
we held together like a rapid running loom weaving
up and down between the other players who held together
stiff as strings as we broke through all their empty
edges. Suddenly it was no game. Perfect harmony
of movement and song. The referee could blow no whistle.
In victory I always refused you
entry. This time
I am going to win.


## Mother

Everytime I leave you
and approach her
she that will give me entry
give me design
Everytime I leave you
hoping to face and touch
warm earth
Everytime when the spell
is so deeply upon me
I hear your voice
 calling me back
 calling me back
not quietly, not softly
not in gentle or happy mourning
but a strident
 "bring him back alive"
 "bring him back alive"
as if you were the Greek mother
from the balustrade of the fortress
pleading to the Senior Officers

that I not go into battle
or, as if, in your eyes
without you, death would be
my one and only
possible
chore. No,
mother. I have left,
though begging, I float
like a swan
over 30
white lakes.


## Requiem

I watch the roses float
upon the sea
a wreath
for my mother her bosom
unleashing all that was given
all that was forbidden
her four sons, my father
and me


## The Song of This House

It's November
and I have the first hole
ever in the sole
of my left, big brown boot.
It's November
and I have to junk the car
the transmission is shot
beyond repair. It's November
and I'm chanting
I want love I want love
We've swept the dust
out of the house
cleaned all the laundry
ordered dry goods,

vegetables and chickens.
And I am screaming
I want love I want love
I open my heart
like the slippery pages
of the telephone book
numbers I am full of numbers
and addresses and Cities
all over the Bay
and I am breathing
I want love I want love
Bottle of glue, key chain
all these passionless objects
that surround a body
full of blood beating, flesh
attentive and hungry
and I'm moaning
and groaning I want love
I want love. The moon
is in retreat the sun
left hanging my typewriter
falls thru the desk
down down I follow it
I follow it into the night
into the dark I am lost
Where are you
It's November
and I'm waiting


**Floor: O**

*from* **Elevator Landscapes**

On this floor
there are no numbers.
We walk out
beyond their civilisation.
Five kangaroos, four of them
are coupling
each other. The fifth

nods that we enter
them like fresh meat
into lovely sandwiches.
I'm drawn to your couple,
you're drawn to mine.
We are not at war
with each other.
I'm just rolling and rocking
between two kangaroos
that love every inch
of my body. They take me
to a rubbing heighth
until there is a low
moaning sound
out of my belly
like the whistling wail
across a telegraph wire
crazing a message
thru the middle
of winter. I cannot hear you
but hear you scream
with malevolent delight.
My mind zeroes
into a searing blank.
I come out of it
pouring the sound
of white juice.
My kangaroo lovers
liberating me
from their hot brown
fur. We meet each other
cleansed from a new light
as the fifth kangaroo
rubs an empty pouch
and nods us
back in thru
those open doors.

**Floor: Five**

*from* **Elevator Landscapes**

She does not talk.
I pull my left
shoulder back.
I carry an orange
in my left
arm pit. She has
a bird in the cage
of her back. The two
are in the middle
of a conversation.
Orange to bird. Bird
to orange. I am
deeply jealous. My lips
are sealed
like sour artichokes.

# Ian Young

It's no good
being an actor:
always getting a walk-on part in
somebody's cheap nightmare . . .

In the blackness,
with you
enclosed in your dark
sleeping,
I can't tell
if the right scenery
is being wheeled into your mind
or know what harmless monsters
inhabit your cute doll's head.

Is Nureyev
always dancing
behind your eyes
or old movies
rerun endlessly
inside your brain?

Who then?
Who would your naked hands invent
from the dream?
Who
would be Big Madonna?
Caesar (a trifle magenta perhaps)?
Christ, in a paper outfit?

I dunno.
It is not me I think.
(That
was someone else's idea.)

## Elephants from the Sea

In a Chinese window
of a store on Yonge Street,
I saw a row of green jade elephants,
all carved from one bar of jade
by the delicate hand of the carver —
larger and large elephants,
and young ones hooked along behind;
there was a whole elephant family —
so polished, and green, and smooth,
it seemed as if they'd loomed
from some sleeping forest
under the sea,
and only yesterday had wandered ashore
to find themselves
in a world of gigantic cushioncovers,
and enormous bamboo fans.


## The Skull

When the boy undressed,
I saw on his left shoulder
a blue tattoo —
two daggers, crossed
under a skull.
"That's pretty phony,"
he said, and laughed,
uncertain.
Later, I half expected it
to peel off
in my mouth.

## A Sugar-Candy Bird

In bed
with my friend's young brother,
a boy of sixteen:
his penis
swelled
so big and thick
I thought it would
              split
like a ripe pod,
or those glazed
and gaudy candy-birds
from Mexico —
              break
suddenly open,
and spill
white sugar dust
over us both.


## Double Exposure

At a party of university people
Jimmy and I sat on a bed
that seemed to be floating.
The whisky-drinkers
were making identical comments,
dancing ever so slowly,
and eyeing each other.
One girl had put Christmas ornaments
on her ears,
and a long-haired kid
read poems at the walls.

I was watching Jimmy —
his hands
holding a towel
and a book of Prevert —
his bare legs
and the curve of his prick
under the cut-down jeans.
The people all looked at us,
their mouths open,
and began to fade away
just as our bed drifted out the window.

They were waving goodbye
as I took pictures of Jimmy
with an imaginary camera.


## At Rochdale

In bed.
My hand on Mark's bare chest,
his fateful thumb round my wrist

used to grip the rubber phallus handle
on a wooden sword:
Macbeth or Macduff — which was it?
          (Smith was the other)

It was all smiles then.

Later the hookah caterpillar
ate big holes in your mind:
Strange days.
People who weren't there:    "Hello"
      "Pleased to meet you"

Talking at impossible angles
under the silence
: sitting
in the Psychiatric, peeling
flakes of paint . . .
"They give you tobacco"    (noddy laugh    laugh)

Just once,
coming out of the gay club:
"Is there somewhere we can go?
. . . a friend's place?"
Holding hands on the street . . .

"Want to come and take pictures Mark?"

(wait a while):

"No . . . That doesn't excite me man . . .
Turn over.
Let me feel your back and ass.

"Man, everything is so profound . . ."

# Biographical Notes

## Milton Acorn

"I was born in a small province, Prince Edward Island, somewhere about the same time as Jack Benny. I like to call myself an Indian, with some justification (the poems and biographical sketches about me invariably refer to me as "red" — it means more than my ruddy color and even more than my politics). I am also Scots, Welsh, Portuguese, not in that order and with some damnable English too . . . which I have spent my life denying. I simplify it by saying I'm a thousandth generation Canadian. There is such a thing and from it Canadians can take assurance that their nation really does exist.

"I worked as a carpenter for many years, but the alienated conditions in the trade (though I was a good carpenter) drove me to nervous breakdown. I in fact had published some poems while a carpenter; but the necessity (being a Canadian fully indoctrinated with the work ethic) of justifying my existence entailed me then becoming a good poet. I'm Old Left, merging on New — have sometimes been accused of being anarchist. The Allan Gardens Free Speech Fight, and Georgia Straight are both in part my doing. Unlike most of the Canadian Left I can point to some successes; but what does that mean while millions still starve? Nevertheless it has been that factor of success in my political work which has led to accusations of anarchism. In order to be a good Canadian Leftist you have to be a total failure.

"Was influenced in mid-career by Charles Olson's *Projective Verse*. However I was equally influenced by my own study of poetic history, which revealed that the good poets wrote about the concerns which involved most people.

Their highest concerns. Also I have studied imagery intensely, learning that the secret of imagery is *looking at things with your own eyes.* Also the line and the voice are much my concern. Also the void — not saying too much — leaving gaps and vistas down which the reader can look with his own imagic eyes . . . ."

## Margaret Atwood

"The real truth is unprintable and the rest sounds like a travelogue. I don't know where I'll be living or what I'll be doing when the book comes out, but right now I'm living in England and writing fiction. Other places I've lived: Boston, Toronto, Montreal, Vancouver, Edmonton. As it says on book-backs, I really did grow up in the bush (forest, etc.) in northern Que. and Ontario."
*Books: The Circle Game,* Contact Press, 1966; *The Animals in That Country, Atlantic* / Little, Brown, 1969; *The Journals of Susanna Moodie,* Oxford Univ. Press, 1970; *The Edible Woman, Atlantic* / Little, Brown, 1970 (novel); *Procedures For Underground, Atlantic* / Little, Brown, 1970; *Power Politics,* House of Anansi, 1971.

## Ken Belford

Ken Belford lives in the bush in British Columbia (Smithers, B.C.). He's been a lumberman and worked on a trapline. Last year he got a Canadian Council Grant to write, so . . . that's what he's doing.

His advice about reading his poems is to "try to go into them."

## George Bowering

"Born mountains of BC Dec. 1937; education is western Greyhound bus stations and colleges, mainly UBC, Vancouver, early sixties; air force photographer sometimes looking out of planes too low late fifties. Founding editor of Tish, now editor of Imago & Beaver Kosmos Folios. To have two separate "Selected Poems" published in eastern and western Canada this year. Also going to have my novel, *Mirror on the Floor* filmed this year or next. Governor General's award in poesy for 69. At the moment trying to take major change in life, follow Olson's advice to get away from slop of existentialism, renew my eyes and will as source of history, no force entrapping us. Also influenced by Greg Curnoe, Heraklitus, Albert Ayler, Phil Whalen, William Eastlake. Soon to edit collection of Canadian poems to be published California. Am highranking officer of Nihilist Party of Canada."


## Aram Boyajian

"I want to hear and feel in my poems heartbeats and breath. That is where poetry came from, from the sounds of our own bodies.

"When I read a poet, I can hear him breathe. When I read a great poet, I can see the hairs in his nose rise and fall as he speaks.

"Also, I would like my poetry to capture the heartbeats of what we once were — horses with tremendous hearts full of blood, birds with hearts beating at incredible speeds and fish in the cold water dropping eggs, discharging sperm.

"There is the heartbeat of the lover — and that is why sex is so important in my poems. If I joke about it, that's because I find all the positions of sex quite hilarious.

"Finally, there is the stopping of the heart. Silence. Death. The space between words and lines.

"We are all uneasy, because we are passing through a time when we are preparing ourselves to become murderers. We will end up justifying murder — each and every one of us. The Blacks, the left, the right, the poor, the rich — no matter. Each one will find a reason to kill.

"My poems are against all killers — especially the ones with good reason.

"My parents made their hearts beat like mad sometime in February 1922. I was born on October 26th, 1922, in New York City. I recently completed a film on the poet William Blake with Allen Ginsberg reading the poetry of Blake."

## Harley Elliott

"I was born July 29, 1940, in Mitchell, South Dakota, and moved shortly thereafter to Kansas, where I've spent most of my life. Lived one year (63–64) in Las Vegas, New Mexico getting an MA in painting and, while there, went to a poetry reading by Edward Dorn. Although I had been writing (to use the word kindly) for a number of years, I date that moment as the time I realized what poetry can be, and do, in its full strength. Began to read new poets, rediscover past ones, and train myself in the art of keeping the brain in blossom. Writing ever since, and I hope it never stops.

"I now live in Syracuse, New York, where I divide my time between a wife, daughter, writing, painting, schemes to get back west, attempts to put my Self in order, and all sorts of foolishness."
*Books: Dark Country,* The Crossing Press, 1971.


## Doug Fetherling

Doug Fetherling lives in Toronto where he is active as poet, fiction writer, journalist, editor, broadcaster and columnist. His books of poetry are *The United States of Heaven* (House of Anansi, 1968, and *Our Man in Utopia (Macmillan, 1971).* Twenty-three years old, he has also done critical and bibliographical work on certain American writers of the 1920s, particularly Ben Hecht, the novelist and screen writer.


## Ray Fraser

"I was born in Chatham, New Brunswick, grew up there, leaving when I was 22. I lived in Belleisle, N.B., for one year (as a high school teacher), then headed for Montreal where I've been most of the time since. My employment in Montreal included one year as copy editor and staff writer for *Midnight,* three years as a free lancer (mostly for *Midnight*), and this past year I've been on a Canada Council grant. There's a year missing somewhere, but I don't know where it went.

"In 1965 or '66 I co-founded *Intercourse* magazine, and edited and published most of the 14 issues which have appeared to date. I have three books of poems published and a novel "The Robin Hood Gang" due out in the Spring of '71. I have a second novel written, prepared to come out after the first. One way or another I will have a fourth book of poems out soon. I've had one play produced in Montreal and published some short stories in assorted little magazines. Also the occasional essay, not to mention some redoubtable editorials in *Intercourse*.

"I am the First Vice-President of the Canadian Chapter of the Flat Earth Society.

"I write my poems for people who are at least semi-literate; what's good enough for the novelist is good enough for the poet. I am against the concept of poetry being the preserve of a self-styled literary elite. For me real poetry is a live body that talks and moves, not a corpse laid out for dissection. Strangely enough, many alleged poets prefer to work with corpses; these are the ones I get bad reviews from. I also get good reviews and that's as it should be. But good or bad, I haven't noticed that reviews make any difference in the number of persons who will buy a book of poems. That's because it's been instilled into the majority of people that poems are corpses to be dissected, and they don't consider themselves competent pathologists, or pathologists at all, or are even interested in the profession. I expect things to improve."

**Len Gasparini**

"Born 1941, Windsor, Ontario (across the river from Detroit). I dropped out of high-school in 1958; thus began my interminable Wanderjahr of hitch-hiking and unemployment. Desperate, I joined the U.S. Navy in 1962; was chronically A.W.O.L. till discharged in 1964. I've been a salesman, truck-driver, farm hand, taxicab-driver, journalist, and factory worker. My first poem was published in 1967. Co-edited a little mag, *Mainline,* the following year. Received a Canada Council short term grant in 1969. I am an active member of the League of Canadian Poets, and take part in poetry readings. My first book of poetry, *Cutty Sark,* was published in 1970. I have also edited the Collected Poems of Bertram Warr.

"My only theory of poetry *is* poetry. I spend as much time reading and listening to poetry as I do writing it. Words are my tools, and working with them requires ecstasy, energy, and concentration; or, as Hart Crane (my favorite poet) put it: "One must be drenched in words, literally soaked with them to have the right ones form themselves into the proper pattern at the right moment." I believe that imagination is the soul of the poet.

"At present I live in Windsor with my wife and two children."


## John Gill

John Gill was born in Chicago, Ill., in 1924. Lived there during his childhood; raised really along the shore of Lake Michigan when you could still swim in it. He did the middle-class thing — went to college and from there into teaching (after sitting in Iceland as a radio operator for 18 months during W W II).

After teaching for about a dozen years, he decided he had no great urge to tell anybody anything. The logical move was to write poetry, edit *New: American & Canadian Poetry* magazine and publish New / Books from The Crossing Press which he started with friends. This way he could do and say without the teachers' stigma: role-playing within a system.

He lives in Trumansburg, N.Y. on a 40-acre piece of land where he edits, publishes, writes, and loafs.


## Robert Hershon

"I was born across the street from Mayor Hylan's old brownstone on Bushwick Ave. in Brooklyn in 1936. My family moved to Queens and, after sleeping my way through NYU, I escaped to San Francisco. There, to my astonishment, I began writing things that looked suspiciously like poems. Suspicion lingers. I now live in

Brooklyn again, with my wife, Michaeleen, two very
energetic children and countless pieces of paper pertaining
to *Hanging Loose,* a quarterly of which I am one of the
2,000 known editors."
*Books: Atlantic Avenue,* Unicorn Press, 1970; and three
from New / Books: *Swans Loving Bears Burning the
Melting Deer* (1967). *4-Telling* (with Emmett Jarrett, Dick
Lourie and Marge Piercy, 1971), and *Grocery Lists* (1971).


## Geof Hewitt

"Ambition could be any artist's greatest problem, and is
certainly at war in me. There I am, chasing myself, trying to
kick my own ass, while screaming "GROW!" The ambitious
notion of "career" has to be overhauled to the point where
people are free to be what they want to be — lost efficiency
is no sacrifice to the benefit of a smile.

  "The widespread writing of poetry could be a symptom
that our language has lost its meaning, the attempt, through
juxtaposition, to qualify experience beyond the challenging
simplicity of words, which threaten to be stereotypes —
either because we mistreat them, or because they're not
correctly heard. How many times I've tried to convey in
conversation the excitement of a moment and seeing the
inadequacy of my words, hoped to salvage all with a
desperate "well it was *really exciting!"*

  "The notion of American poetry becomes more
anachronistic when the majority of Americans are apathetic
towards their loss of freedom — "conspiracy" convictions
being a visible harbinger of doom. When society's a prison,
jail seems mild enough, but who will free us when we
cannot see the bars?"
*Books: Poem & Other Poems,* The Kumquat Press, 1966;
*Waking Up Still Pickled,* The Lillabulero Press, 1967;
*Quickly Aging Here* (ed.), Doubleday-Anchor Books, 1969.

## Emmett Jarrett

"I was born in Louisiana in 1939, flunked out of Florida State in 1958, spent a year in Chicago and three in the Army. Have lived in New York since 1962 except for a year in Greece. Since 1967 I've taught at St. Ann's School in Brooklyn.

"Since 1966 I've been a co-editor of *Hanging Loose*. My first book of poems was *The Days* (Beanbag Press, 1968), second and third come from The Crossing: *4-Telling* (with Marge Piercy, Robert Hershon and Dick Lourie) and *Greek Feet* (all mine), both 1971.

"I am married to Carol Baum and we spend a lot of time trying to move to the country.

"Most of my 'statements' about poetry and craft turn out pompous but here goes. I think poetry is still about birth and death, love, anger, fear, tenderness, nature, cities, vision. I try to measure my lines in natural breath units, make my images out of real things, common and uncommon, actual and imagined.

"I think all criticism is necessarily after the fact. When poems sing, they need no explanation. When there is vision, including comic vision which interests me increasingly, there's no need to talk about it. I keep learning, from old poets like Blake, Whitman, Williams, new poets like some friends in this anthology.

"We keep trying and do our best, that's all."


## George Jonas

George Jonas came to Canada from Budapest, Hungary, in 1956 and has been living in Toronto. His first collection of poems, *The Absolute Smile,* appeared in 1967 and his next book, *The Happy Hungry Man,* was published in 1970. Besides poetry, he has written several plays for radio and television. He works as a drama producer for the Canadian Broadcasting Corporation in Toronto.

## Etheridge Knight

Etheridge Knight has spent at least 8½ years in "the joint" . . . a lot of that time spent sort of educating himself . . . and of course Gwendolyn Brooks is one of the people who turned him on to poetry, that is, reading her and Langston. He taught for a while in a black lit program at the University of Pittsburgh. Etheridge Knight says of himself, "I'm not a junkie who writes poetry, but a poet who has used / uses / will not use / junk." He edited *Black Voices from Prison,* Pathfinder Press, New York. *Poems from Prison,* Broadside Press, Detroit, 1968, is his first book of poetry.

## Tom Kryss

"I promise to keep the biographical item you seek before my mind for a few days, and if nothing worthwhile comes by then, you can print the rumors, or run a blank space. A somewhat humorous blade of grass in the shadow of a gallows to you."

## Patrick Lane

Born high in the Kootenay mountains
in small town of Salmo ( I was 27th
in population) moved to coast and back
to Okanagan Valley until I married
in 1958 had three children and all
the time moving around Canada's
northland working as a cat-skinner
mill worker logging truck operator
chokerman chainsawman miner west
coast fishing boats on the bum and
wandering carrying wife and kids with
me farther north worked as First-Aid Man
in isolated northern village
for a year and a half until totally mad
and brother great poet Red Lane died
in 1964 and I moved to Vancouver

where I started *Very Stone House*
with Seymour Mayne Bill Bissett
Jim Brown also co-editing small mag
with Chuck Carlson and working with
Bill Bissett on Blew Ointment Press
Worked *Very Stone House* publishing
best of the west coast writers in Canada
(started renaissance of west coast
movement with press) received first
Canada Council grant in 1967 so wandered
across North America grooving on people
places drugs jail etc back to coast
divorced from wife who left for Africa
and I back to the mountains and living
with Kwakiutl Indians in northern BC
and sawmill work to San Francisco, Yukon
and Toronto / Montreal getting to
Trumansburg (outside Ithaca New York)
where I joined forces with John Gill
and Dick Lourie to start The Crossing
Press to publish best of new Canadian
and American poets — working on two
anthologies of my own and awaiting
receipt of next Canada Council grant
of $4000.00 and then continued publishing
with wandering soul maybe travelling
theatre etc yes.


## Irving Layton

Irving Layton was born in a small town near Bucharest,
Rumania, on March 12, 1912. In the following year his
parents emigrated to Montreal where he lived. He obtained
a B.Sc. from MacDonald College in 1939, served as a
Lieutenant in the Royal Canadian Artillery during the
Second World War, and obtained his M.A. from McGill
University in 1946.

In the 1940s he was associated with *First Statement*
and *Northern Review;* in the 1950s with *CIVn* and *Contact.*
His early books were published by avant-garde and poets'

presses, but since 1959 his books have been issued by a major Canadian publisher, McClelland and Stewart.

In recent years he has been accorded several high honors: a Canada Foundation Fellowship in 1957; a Canada Council award in 1959; the Governor-General's Medal in 1960; and the President's Medal from the University of Western Ontario in 1961. He received another Canada Council award in 1967 which enabled him to visit Israel, India and Nepal and collect the material for his book *The Whole Bloody Bird*. He was Poet-In-Residence at Sir George Williams University, and subsequently Writer-In-Residence at the University of Guelph. In 1970, Bishop's University conferred on him a Doctor of Civil Laws. At present he is a professor in English Literature at York University.

In Canada Layton is known as an outspoken and controversial figure and the debate over the merits of his poetry has been long and vociferous. That he should be read has been stressed by many strong and respected champions in Canada and in the United States. William Carlos Williams wrote: "With his vigor and abilities who shall not say that Canada will not have produced one of the west's most famous poets?" Robert Creeley has suggested that Irving Layton may be the First Great Canadian Poet. The titles of his most recent books are *Periods of the Moon, The Shattered Plinths, The Whole Bloody Bird,* and *Nail Polish.*

## Don L. Lee

*Statement of Action*

"I'm a blackman / African who writes, not a blackman who happens to write. My work, if I'm to be true to myself and my people, should reflect our blackness, our African-ness.

"Everything is political; from the air we breathe to the water that slowly kills us; from the area we live in to the areas we're not allowed to work in. Art (poetry, drama, music, etc.) is political; there is no such thing as apolitical art. Art for art's sake is an invalid concept and belongs back in Greece 400 B.C.; and if you don't believe this, then perhaps, just perhaps you don't know what's happening."

"Poet, Critic, Essayist, Don L. Lee is currently a Lecturer in Afro-American Literature at the University of Illinois, Chicago Circle Campus. His published poetry includes the following volumes: *Think Black; Black Pride; Don't Cry, Scream; We Walk the Way of the New World.* Two new volumes are expected in spring, 1971. One is an in-depth study of the contemporary Black Arts Movement entitled *Dynamite Voices: Black Poets of the 1960's and '70's.* The other is a collection of selected poems from all of his previous volumes as well as new poems, entitled *Directionscore: New and Selected Poems.* All of Mr. Lee's work has been published by Broadside Press, Detroit, Michigan. Other individual poems and essays have appeared in the following publications and others: *Liberator, Freedomways, Black World, New York Times, Muhammad Speaks, Black Scholar, Evergreen Review, Ebony, Chicago Defender.*"

### Lyn Lifshin

"A book: *Why is the House Dissolving?* from Open Skull Press, 1968, probably out of print. Pamphlets coming from Abraxus, Lillabulero, New. Poems in anthologies from Abraxus, Aldebarron Wormwood, Atom Mind, The Lit and poems in three collections of erotic poems, all still untitled. A record taped two summers ago that may someday actually appear from Folkways. Scholastic: *after it all happens again.* Readings at Cornell, Colby, Rensselaer Polytechnical Institute, Wells College, Russell Sage, Wisconsin State etc. A Hart Crane Memorial Award and fellowship at University of Colorado's Writing Conference. Groups of poems coming in Carolina Quarterly, Lillabulero. Cafe Solo, Quartet, Beloit, December, Wormwood, hanging loose, Wisconsin Review, Shaded Windows, Pebble, Red Clay, Red Cedar; A New / Book *Black Apples* from The Crossing Press, 1971 and a yellow car to go anywhere."

## Dick Lourie

"I write for myself and for my tribe — the alternate underground culture / the Movement / the Revolution / us / white black third world indian brothers and sisters / oppressed women and oppressed men / liberated women and liberated men. "Poetry for the Poets" is what had been happening up to say Ginsberg. What I consider myself a part of is the movement away from that, and toward poetry with a broader, tribal constituency.

"Only gradually, over the last ten years, have I become a member of my tribe. It is growing of course all the time; and some of my poems also are intended to recruit as well as to celebrate. That's one reason I have irony as a basic strategy in a lot of my poems. The irony is a doorway you can come through, onto my side. If I bring you far enough or often enough, you might stay, join the tribe.

"I don't like debates about whether poetry can be or ought to be political, or polemic, or propaganda. I think such debates are as useless as the ones about "what is a poem?" — useless because impractical and unnecessary. If it works, let it. If it takes you somewhere, go with it.

"As for biography: overcoming the cultural disadvantagement of a Princeton AB and a Columbia MA, I started as a college teacher and advanced, through music and English, to the pre-school teaching level, and lately have begun full-time work as again a (hopefully better than I used to be) English teacher in the Seventh Grade."

## David McFadden

"My poems are not only for ecstacy but also for discovery and as for me I am like that too.

"I believe in women, the dignity of labor, Greg Curnoe, & the secret unseen unnamed forces of the universe. I am a 30-year-old reporter, married, 2 children, live in Hamilton, Ontario, mild-mannered but impatient, sad-eyed but boyish, a cool exterior but a veritable smoking inferno inside —

"My most recent books are The Great Canadian Sonnet, Coach House Press, and Poems Worth Knowing (soon to come from Coach House Press)."

**Larry Mollin**

Larry Mollin "Lived in the suburbs for eighteen years
building up my body and trying to be somebody. Dreamed
the jock's dream — i was short, but could dribble good, hit
hard, run fast. By the time i graduated i discovered i was
smart and was expected in college on schedule. Still
dreaming, i tried to go Romantic and South but ended up in
Georgetown University School of Foreign Service —
became a foreigner immediately, couldn't keep up with the
college men, so i bought a motorcycle and a new image. Had
a lot of fun trying to kill myself and read poetry to heal the
wounds. Met some actors who seemed to be having a good
time, so i joined in and did two summers of summerstock
on Martha's Vineyard, Mass. Finished up in Ithaca College
B.A. — still no poetry but a lot of good college living. To
New York — teaching to buy time from the Draft — though
it didn't matter. i was too crazy to teach — too crazy to army
— just crazy enough to start writing poetry and act. Saw
the Living Theatre 15 times and left New York for
Theatrecosmos in Trumansburg, New York — a great mixed
media theatre poem which could have worked — zeroed
out! Went North finally to Toronto — a new Canadian, new
candy bars, new cigarettes! and people who grew up on
different TV channels than me! And here i am acting and
directing and doing a lot of writing, especially songs for my
rock 'n' roll brother, Fred. Oh, i have one chapbook of
poems out from New / Books *Which Way to the Egress* and
hepatitis as I write this — "


**John Newlove**

John Newlove was born in Regina in 1938. He has worked
in various parts of Canada & the U.S. as a teacher, radio
announcer and laborer. At present he lives in Toronto and
works as an editor for McClelland & Stewart Publishers.
    His latest books are *Black Night Window,* McClelland
& Stewart, 1968; and *The Cave,* McClelland & Stewart, 1970.

## Alden Nowlan

Alden Nowlan has had 8 books published in Canada — and one in United States, a selected poems, titled *Playing the Jesus Game*. His most recent Canadian book, *Bread, Wine and Salt* won the Governor-General's Award, the equivalent of the Pulitzer Prize. Alden Nowlan has also received a Guggenheim Fellowship & has won two Canada Council grants. He is currently writer-in-residence at the University of New Brunswick, Fredericton, New Brunswick, Canada.

## Robert Peterson

Robert Peterson was born in 1924 in Denver, Colo., and raised in San Francisco. He has published three books of poetry: *Home for the Night* (1962), *The Binnacle* (1967), and *Wondering Where You Are* (1969). For the past two years he has been teaching at Reed College, Portland, Oregon. His home is in Mill Valley, Calif.

"My poems very often begin as stories. But there are always too many characters and too many complications, so I must work at becalming myself. What pleases me most is to find the fine line between tragedy and comedy. It's at such times that I feel I truly understand the speed of light."

## David Phillips

"neil young sings from the living room 'i believe in yu' & Pat is splashing in the bath in this warm house tonight the rain falling outside. a friend has left last night now 3 thousand miles away in toronto where he is, entered again other worlds & did arrive five days before, here into this world with love as we were able to see & enter into. there is no other time but this time we are continually entering & enter our task to get as close as we can. we carry poems around with us read them to each other, enter the poem & are carried. where do we go? we read the poems & talk to each other, doors open & close, jet planes leave the airports, carrying us into & out of each others worlds. i've thot poems were a means of getting us closer to the actualities of our lives. but the poems are not our lives, tho we can take part in the life of the poems. i've noticed first of all there is this pleasure, even if the way is mean & dark or confusing & we cannot be sure of where it is we are being taken, there is this pleasure the poem opens to us, the pleasure moves us in the urge to get closer to its source in ourselves & outside where the poem is made, a bridge being built as we cross it. it is first of all a pleasure to find myself apprenticed in the process of making these bridges, vehicles, poems, whatever name. how else to say it? the poem continues & the need to get as close as possible is the need to write poems is the need to be exactly where we are."


## Marge Piercy

"I was born and raised in a workingclass neighborhood of little wooden houses in Detroit. Since escaping — social mobility via the university and then dropping out to preserve what remained of who I was — I've lived in Chicago, Boston, San Francisco, Brooklyn, Manhattan. Now I am about to try living in the country, in a house on the edge of a marsh in Cape Cod. I will cough away from air pollution if I stay simmering any longer in New York. I'd like some quiet space for a while, to repair and fill gaps and think a little further on than the next crisis. I am political as thoroughly as I am alive or female and don't anticipate opting out of the struggle. My first, my strongest identification now is with women's liberation, but I still feel a larger connection to the Movement in general.

"Since high school I have been writing poems and novels, which are as different kinds of animals as crows and chipmunks, though I guess themes run from one to the other at times. As a political writer I get bagged often as less serious, less real, more faddish than people who write about their wives or their last Fulbright trip. But any poem that contains a social attitude is political. Getting published has been a long battle for me. If what I write touches you, use it in good health."

*Publications:* Poetry: *Breaking Camp,* Wesleyan Univ.

Press, 1968; *Hard Loving*, Wesleyan Univ. Press, 1969; *4-Telling* (with Bob Hershon, Emmett Jarrett, Dick Lourie) New / Books, The Crossing, 1971; Fiction: *Going Down Fast*, Trident, 1969; *Dance the Eagle to Sleep*, Doubleday, 1970.

## J. D. Reed

J. D. Reed "was born before Aquarius in Michigan. He's cried like a baby ever since. After a year of drinking on a Guggenheim Fellowship, he's secured a job as an Ass't Professor at UMass beginning Sept., 1971. My move has been away from 'product identification' in poetry — Things — toward a mystical, muse-ridden view of experience. I am attracted by the Great Impurists: Rilke, Neruda, Apollinaire and Vallejo. 'One shrivels from a sociological concept of the universe and returns to song — imperfect accurate and strong.' Song and Sound endure: revolutions pass like Russian roulette."
Book: *Express Ways*, poems by J. D. Reed, Simon & Schuster, 1969.

## Dennis Saleh

"I was born in Chicago in 1942, and moved to Fresno, California in 1948. Lived there from then on, going to school at Fresno State College, until I left for a year in school in Arizona. After deciding what I was studying there wasn't going to work out — psychology, I went to UC Irvine for two years, and got a writing degree. Began teaching in the UC system then, doing modern poetry and poetry writing, and have been for three years, most recently at Santa Cruz; ran a reading series the three years too. Married, one son. I've been publishing poems in magazines for about five years now, and have a book of them done. Have also co-edited a book that kept disappearing into the future, but will finally be published Summer, 1971 — *Just what the country needs Another Poetry Anthology*."

## Tom Schmidt

"Born San Francisco, 1939. Grew up Albany, across bay beside Berkeley. Back to S.F., including Writing Program, S.F. State, 56–64, on and off. Music, Army, Mexico, marriage, teaching American River College in Sacramento, writing, Greater Carmichael Traveling Street Band w/Bro. Lee Love. Now living with wife, Maria, two cats, Manuela & Beliza, Fair Oaks, Calif., near the American River. Also write stories (*Transatlantic Review* #37; James T. Phelan Award for Short Fiction, 1970), make translations from Spanish (*Modern Poetry in Translation* (London) #'s 7 & 10), essays ("Tom Schmidt at Folsom Prison," in *Works,* vol. II, # 4).

"About poetry: I am thinking of a column of air lifted above the earth, levered from the plant of the feet by the legs, hamstring, guts. A column of air surrounded by the lungs and throat and mouth, watched by eyes in the mind. Sometimes the column of air is stretched by machines. Suppose I play the clarinet. My fingers tremble above the column of air. Music, 'the purest art.' I want poems on the same column of air, now stretched by words. My fingers tremble above the naked column of air. Poems levered off the earth, a column of air lifted from the plant of the feet, watched by eyes in the mind."


## John Oliver Simon

"born 4/21/42, NYC. Putney School, Swarthmore, UC Berkeley, yellow cab, hitching Mideast + europe, guerilla printer + street poetry, edit Aldebaran Review, brown belt in Goju Karate, 2 daughters, Lorelei and Kiakima.
Books: Roads to Dawn Lake (Oyez 68), Adventures of the Floating Rabbi (Runcible Spoon 68), Cat Pome (Gunrunner Press 69), Dancing Bear (Undermine Press 69), The Woodchuck Who Lives on Top of Mt. Ritter (Galactic Approximation 70), Picture of a Red Bull Striding on Its Hind Legs into Forest Bearing an Empty Field of Words (Oyez 71). working on a science-fiction novel about the poet-hero Bruno Levy.

"politics comes from the earth + finds strength + judgment there. poetry comes from the pre-human earth, walking thru it, the self alone on my-our entangling journey. particularly important in time of pre-extinction to hold to the real "as dwarf-pine clutches rock" — maybe a time of revolution, in which case the commitment to sense and animal is totally necessary as everyone round takes turns at playing Stalin"


## Stephen Vincent

"Born 1941, grew up in Richmond, California, lunch bucket industrial town on San Francisco Bay. Education: Anglo-European grapple for too many years (U.C., Riverside, the Sorbonne, M.A., Creative Writing, S.F. State). Peace Corps, Nigeria, 1965–67. Since then, mainly in San Francisco, learning ritual & movement at Ann Halprin's Dancers' Workshop & John Robinson's God's Eye Theater. Also teaching English all over town, Chinese emigrants, State students and, most recently, leading creative writing workshops in high schools and getting together a course, Bay Area Poetry & Painting since WWII, that I will teach this spring at the S.F. Art Institute.

"I want the poetry I write to merge from all the perceptions that happen from behind the veneer or mask of all previous situations, whether the school, the family, the streets, lovers, dreams the political condition. (Yes, for the sake of the country, Free All Political Prisoners). The process: the language bent and beat close to music (jazz, blues, rock), shaped according to a particular knowledge of ritual, both African & American, and, of course, a precise sense of what is possible in English, the tone & rhythm available to each syllable within the context of each new poem. I want the whole process to be a logical centering of all the disparate forces that work to unwind us both as individuals and as a culture(s). Naturally it involves working towards a new vision of who and where we are. Finally, as they say, I want a poem to get it, get us on. The red star on the garbage can lid that flied away in the morning & turns gold in the night flying over the wheat of our each and every Kansas. Who am I? Recently saying good bye to Tom Sawyer and who are you and what have you been doing, lately?"

## Ian Young

Ian Young was born in London, England, in 1945, and lives in Scarborough, Ontario, Canada.

He has published four books of poetry: *White Garland: 9 Poems for Richard, Year of the Quiet Sun, Double Exposure,* and *Cool Fire: 10 Poems by Ian Young & Richard Phelan,* as well as a translation of Count Fersen's *Curieux d'Amour.*

His poems and essays appear in the anthologies *T.O. Now: The Young Toronto Poets, Notes for a Native Land, Poets of Canada 1969, Fifteen Winds, Printed Matter* and *Storm Warnings,* and in various periodicals.

# Acknowledgments

The editor is grateful to the poets themselves for permission to publish their copyrighted poems. Many of the poems in this anthology were first published in magazines; some appeared in books by the individual poets. Grateful acknowledgment is made to the following:

For Milton Acorn to Ryerson Press (Toronto) and the author; for Margaret Atwood to *Blew Ointment, Canadian Forum, Kayak, New Work, Poetry*, House of Anansi Press (Toronto), and the author; for Ken Belford to *Prism International*, Very Stone House (Vancouver), and the author; for George Bowering to House of Anansi Press (Toronto), *Imago*, Quarry Press (Kingston, Ontario), and the author; for Aram Boyajian to *NEW: American and Canadian Poetry, Pyramid*, and the author; for Harley Elliott to *Back Door, Hanging Loose, NEW: American and Canadian Poetry, Trace*, NEW / BOOKS, The Crossing Press (Trumansburg, New York), and the author; for Doug Fetherling: "Dialogue 4 1 Voice Only," "She Employed the Familiar Tu Form," "Sex Play in Four Acts" from *The United States of Heaven*, House of Anansi Press (Toronto) © 1968 by Doug Fetherling. All others from *Our Man in Utopia*, Macmillan © 1971 by Doug Fetherling; for Ray Fraser to *Delta Canada*, Poverty Press, and the author; for Len Gasparini to Quarry Press and the author; for John Gill to *Hearse*, NEW / BOOKS, The Crossing Press (Trumansburg, New York), and the author; for Robert Hershon to *Chicago Review, Hanging Loose, NEW: American and Canadian Poetry*, NEW / BOOKS, The Crossing Press (Trumansburg, New York), and the author; for Geof Hewitt to *NEW: American and Canadian Poetry*, The Lillabulero Press, and the author; for Emmett Jarrett to *Chicago Review, NEW: American and Canadian Poetry, New York Quarterly*, Beanbag Press, Viking Press, and the author; for George Jonas to House of Anansi Press (Toronto), and the author; for Etheridge Knight to *Motive, The Black World*, Broadside Press, and the author; for Tom Kryss to *Death Row, Runcible Spoon*, Open Skull Press, Second Aeon Publications, and the author; for Patrick Lane to NEW / BOOKS, The Crossing Press (Trumansburg, New York), Very Stone House (Vancouver), and the author; for Irving Layton to McClelland &

Stewart (Toronto), and the author; for Don L. Lee to Broadside Press
(Detroit, Michigan) for permission to reprint poetry from *Black Pride*
© Copyright 1968 by Don L. Lee, *Don't Cry, Scream* © Copyright 1969
by Don L. Lee, *Think Black* © Copyright 1969 by Don L. Lee, and
*We Walk the Way of the New World* © Copyright 1970 by Don L. Lee;
for Lyn Lifshin to *Abraxus, Hearse, Work,* NEW / BOOKS, The
Crossing Press (Trumansburg, New York), Open Skull Press, and the
author; for Dick Lourie to *NEW: American and Canadian Poetry,
Poems of the People,* Unicorn Press, and the author; for David
McFadden to *Canadian Forum, Hyphid, Intrepid, Quarry,* Coach
House Press (Toronto), McClelland & Stewart (Toronto), and the
author; for Larry Mollin to *Earthwords,* NEW / BOOKS, The Crossing
Press (Trumansburg, New York), and the author; for John Newlove to
Contact Press (Toronto), Fiddlehead Books, The Ryerson Press, and the
author; for Robert Peterson to Bindweed Press (San Francisco), Kayak
Books (San Francisco), Lillabulero Press (Ithaca, New York), and the
author; for David Phillips to Coach House Press (Toronto),
Talonbooks (Vancouver), and the author; for Marge Piercy to *Diane,
Hearse, NEW: American and Canadian Poetry, Up From Under,* and
the author; for J. D. Reed to *Sumac,* Baleen Press (Phoenix, Arizona),
and the author; for Dennis Saleh to *Kayak, Massachusetts Review,
NEW: American and Canadian Poetry, New Orleans Review, North
American Review,* and the author; for Tom V. Schmidt to *Chelsea,
Field, Leviathan, NEW: American and Canadian Poetry, Steps,
Viewpoints,* and the author; for John Oliver Simon to Galactic
Approximation Press, Oyez Press, Undermine Press, and the author;
for Stephen Vincent to *NEW: American and Canadian Poetry,*
NEW / BOOKS, The Crossing Press (Trumansburg, New York), and
the author; and for Ian Young to House of Anansi Press (Toronto),
NEW / BOOKS, The Crossing Press (Trumansburg, New York), and
the author.